Beginner's Guide to

# Bricklaying

Beginner's Guide to

# Bricklaying

R. A. Daniel

Heinemann : London

William Heinemann Ltd
10 Upper Grosvenor Street, London W1X 9PA

LONDON   MELBOURNE   JOHANNESBURG   AUCKLAND

First published 1986

© William Heinemann Ltd 1986

ISBN 0 434 90302 7

Made and printed in Great Britain by
R. J. Ackford Ltd, Chichester

# Preface

Bricklaying is a very ancient craft which has survived many changes in building methods and seen the introduction of countless new materials. Many times these 'new' methods and materials have been confidently predicted to replace brickwork but always the brick has survived, either ousting the newcomer or being used in conjunction with it.

In the 1960s factory-made precast concrete buildings were going to take the place of brickwork but the brick is still the preferred material for most domestic construction and is being increasingly chosen by architects as the cladding for some of the most prestigious buildings.

Developments in all types of concrete have given rise to a big variety of concrete blocks which have added a new dimension to the work of the bricklayer and introduced new although similar skills. The combination of brick and blockwork looks like continuing as the main structural and cladding materials for the foreseeable future and constantly a new generation of craftsmen will practise the skills.

With increasing leisure time more and more people are gaining satisfaction and pleasure from doing it themselves and turning to trowel work. This book is designed to encourage them to try their skill and aptitude and help them to produce a satisfying piece of work. Apprentices and trainees starting to learn the trade will find the book a very useful introduction.

R. A. D.

# Contents

1  Tools                              1
2  Materials                         15
3  Building the walls                36
4  Work below d.p.c.                 49
5  Scaffolding                       61
6  External walls                    67
7  Pavings and steps                 90
8  Freestanding walls and piers      96
9  Patio and flower boxes           109
10 Pointing a wall                  115
11 Circular paving                  119
12 Garden seat and barbecue         121
13 Feature fireplace                125
14 Garage and utility room          129
   Index                            140

# 1

# **Tools**

The bricklayer's tool kit need not be extensive but certainly the tools must be of good quality as they have to stand up to very hard work. Cheap poor quality tools are always a waste of money because they have a very short life.

### Laying trowels

These vary in shape and use throughout the world but the fact that British bricklayers invariably win the medals at international competitions indicates that the two British trowels and their methods of use are superior to most other types. The main difference between the two British trowels – the London and Northern (Fig. 1) – is that the London trowel does not have a steel ferrule on the end of the handle and the blade is narrower. While the experienced bricklayer can use a trowel 300 mm long with ease it is recommended that the beginner should start off with a 200 mm long trowel. A trowel for a right-handed person is tempered harder on the right and may be slightly rounded on that edge. The opposite side is tempered for the left-handed bricklayer.

Picking up mortar with the trowel correctly is important because a good even trowelful will spread more easily. Do not overload the spot board, but leave room at the side to the left if you are right-handed or to the right if left-handed. Cut some mortar from the heap and draw it to the side of

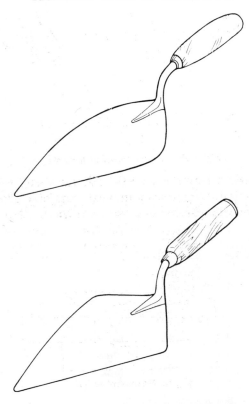

*Fig. 1.* (above) *London pattern trowel.* (below) *Northern pattern trowel*

the board shaping the mortar so that when picked up it will fill the trowel (Fig. 2). The mortar is placed on the wall by drawing the arm back sharply while twisting the wrist at the same time; this action may prove rather difficult for beginners to master and a great deal of practice may be required to achieve a smooth unified action. After spreading the mortar along part of the wall it is then furrowed by drawing the trowel point along it at a fairly flat angle

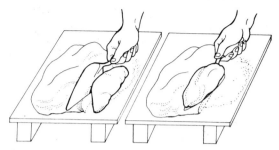

*Fig. 2. Picking up a trowelful of mortar*

(Fig. 3a). Mortar overhanging the side can then be cut off (Fig. 3b); this is the mortar for the next cross joint. The cross joint is applied to the front or back header face depending

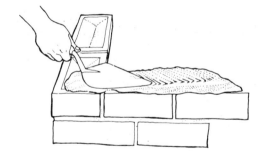

*Fig. 3a. Spreading the bed*

*Fig. 3b. Cutting off the surplus at the edge*

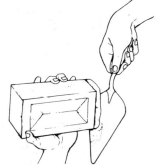

*Fig. 4. Applying the crossjoint*

which way you are working (Fig. 4). To apply a joint to the stretcher or long face the brick must be held and mortar applied as shown in Fig. 5. If the mortar has been spread properly, the brick will only need pressing down on to the

*Fig. 5. Applying the crossjoint to the stretcher face*

bed with a light tap down with the edge of the trowel to firm it into place. Remember to always use the tempered edge for this operation. When spreading mortar the bricklayer should stand facing half left or half right depending in which

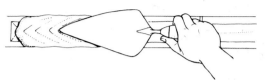

*Fig. 6a. Spreading the mortar bed*

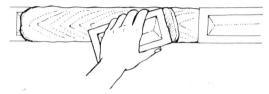

*Fig. 6b. Laying the brick*

direction the work is progressing (Fig. 6a). The diagram refers to a right-handed person, a left-hander must reverse the positions. When laying the brick, the feet should face the wall (Fig. 6b).

## Lump hammer and bolster chisel

Soft bricks and blocks can be cut by striking with the tempered edge of the trowel, but this is not good practice as it is hard on the trowel and is not very accurate. The best way to cut a brick is with a lump hammer and bolster chisel (Fig. 7). Mark the position of the cut with a carpenter's pencil after measuring, or by using a cutting gauge made from wood (Fig. 8). One hard sharp blow with the hammer is best, but some hard bricks may need several hammer blows. To get a good even cut on both faces of the brick the bolster chisel should be struck hard enough to mark the brick surface but not to break it. Repeat on the opposite face then turn the brick back to the first position and cut it

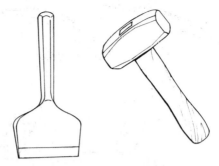

*Fig. 7. Lump hammer and bolster chisel*

with a hard strike on the chisel. If the brick does not cut cleanly through then it may have to be dressed level using a comb hammer.

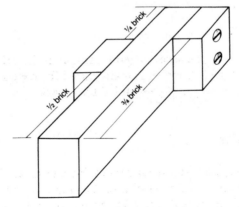

*Fig. 8. Brick cutting gauge*

## Comb hammer or skutch

The comb hammer, Fig. 9 (left), is used for all kinds of cutting work where the bolster chisel has not cut the brick

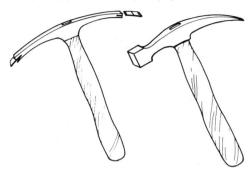

*Fig. 9.* (left) *Comb hammer or skutch.* (right) *Brickhammer*

evenly right through and for fine cutting work. When the steel combs have worn down, new ones can be fitted in the end slots.

## Brick hammer

The bricklayer's general-purpose hammer is the brick hammer, Fig. 9 (right), which is mainly used for rough cutting, plumbing, nailing and general hammer work.

## Line and pins

The bricklaying line is wound on to line pins (Fig. 10) which are pressed into the crossjoint of the course which is to be built. The line must be pulled tight and wound down on to the blade of the pin so that the line is located exactly on the top arris or edge of the brick or block.

An alternative to line pins is line blocks (Fig. 11a). These do not leave any pin-holes or line marks in facing work and can be used on profiles or when working between concrete columns (Fig. 11b). If the line breaks or is accidentally cut

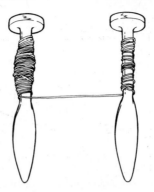

*Fig. 10. Line and line pins*

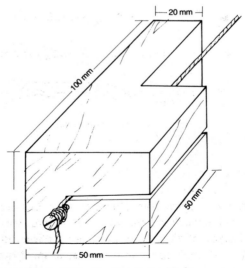

*Fig. 11a. Corner line block*

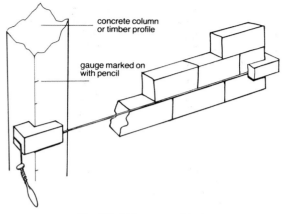

*Fig. 11b. Using corner blocks*

it should be joined with a splice not a knot. The method of splice jointing a line is shown in Fig. 12.

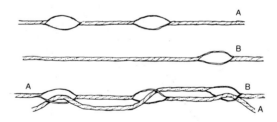

*Fig. 12. Splicing a broken line*

## Plumb level

The bricklayer's spirit level (Fig. 13) is an essential tool to ensure that the work is kept level and plumb. It is 1 metre long and made of either box or girder section aluminium. In its cheapest form, there are two plastic spirit tubes (with bubbles), one set into the level across one end for plumbing, and the other set into the centre for levelling. More robust levels of similar construction, but with plumbing tubes top and bottom and level tubes for using either side are also available.

In addition to plumbing and levelling work, the spirit level is used for checking the alignment of bricks on the face plane when building a corner. The bubbles are not used as the level is only acting as a straight edge.

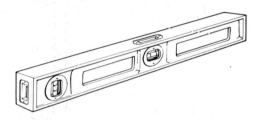

*Fig. 13. Bricklayer's spirit level*

To check a level for accuracy it should be set on a flat surface and the ends of the level marked on the surface with a pencil and the position of the bubble accurately noted. The level should then be reversed and set down in exactly the same position on the pencil lines, where the bubble should be in exactly the same position as it was before it was reversed. To check the level for plumb, first drive two nails into a convenient fixed vertical timber, and plumb the lower nail against the top nail by using a metal plumb bob and line, tapping the lower nail into the wood until perfectly plumb. The spirit level can now be checked by holding it against the nails (Fig. 14). As an alternative, the level can be held against a door frame or something similar and reversed as described for checking the level.

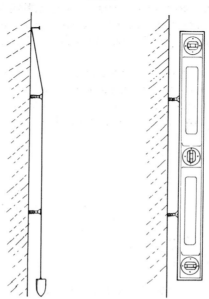

*Fig. 14. Checking for plumb*

## Other tools

Other tools needed by the beginner include setting out and mortar joint finishing tools, which are dealt with in Chapters 4 and 10 respectively. Other hand tools used by the brick-layer are more specialized and not really needed by the novice.

## Equipment

Among essential items of equipment needed for brickwork are buckets – rubber or heavy gauge industrial plastic are long lasting – shovel, wheelbarrow, spot boards, a wooden

*Fig. 15. Builder's shovel*

setting out square, and a gauge rod straight edge. A pressed-steel builder's shovel is suitable for mixing and working mortar and concrete, but a heavier forged steel spade is better for digging and similar harder work (Fig. 15).

The builder's wheelbarrow has a steel body which is capable of standing up to heavy use and rough site conditions. Although a wheelbarrow with solid rubber wheels is cheaper than one with pneumatic tyred wheels, it is more difficult to push on rough site work. Where the ground is soft, or rough

*Fig. 16. Builder's wheelbarrow*

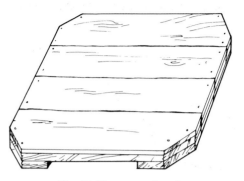

*Fig. 17. Mortar spot board*

and stony, a barrow run of planks will be necessary to enable a person to push a barrow on site. An empty barrow can be trailed behind the person using it, but a loaded barrow must be pushed in order to keep control and steer it. The barrow should always be loaded nearer the front so that the centre of gravity is as close to the wheel as possible and the load on the handles kept to a minimum (Fig. 16).

The mortar spot board can be made from a piece of 12 mm marine plywood 600 × 600 mm square with the corners cut off; or made up of boards with battens screwed to the back

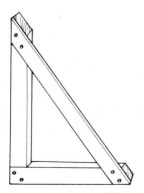

*Fig. 18. Builder's square*

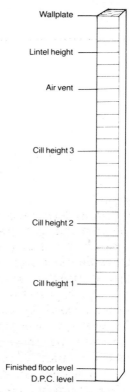

Wallplate

Lintel height

Air vent

Cill height 3

Cill height 2

Cill height 1

Finished floor level
D.P.C. level

*Fig. 19. Example of a marked up gauge rod*

(Fig. 17). Do not use hardboard or thin sheet steel as they will sag in the middle. The wooden setting out square is made up as shown in Fig. 18 with arms at least 600 mm long out of 75 × 20 mm timber. The gauge rod is also made from 75 × 20 mm timber with saw marks set out and measured to show the height of each course of bricks or blocks and positions of sills, lintels, etc. (Fig. 19). Methods of using the setting out square and gauge rod are described in later chapters.

# 2

# Materials

## Bricks

Bricks are made in various ways using a wide variety of natural materials. Pressed and extruded, machine-made types dominate the market, but there are still some hand-made facing bricks; despite their high cost, their characteristic crease marks and irregularities both of shape and colour make them particularly attractive.

Calcium silicate bricks are made by reacting a mixture of lime and silica sand with steam under pressure in an autoclave. They are suitable for a wide range of structures.

Taking into account the variety of materials used, the different methods of manufacture, including firing, the use of additives and surface treatments, there is around 1500 different bricks from which to choose the ones most suitable for the project in hand.

Of course, all bricks are not suitable for all jobs, for instance, the Fletton is an economical and widely available product which is suitable and durable for general walling, but like any other ordinary quality common and facing brick, it can suffer frost damage when used in severely exposed parts of a wall.

Situations which are most susceptible to this kind of damage are those where the brickwork becomes saturated as in the case of retaining walls, free-standing garden walls which have no copings, parapet walls, external steps and pavings.

Always check, either with your supplier or directly with the maker, that the bricks you have chosen are suitable for the project you are to carry out.

## Brick classification

Clay bricks are classified in British Standard 3921:1974 under three varieties:

*Common:* this term does not imply any lack of performance, it simply means that they are not particularly attractive in appearance. They are used below ground level, for the inner leaf of a cavity wall or a partition wall where appearance is not of prime importance.

*Facing:* these bricks are specially made or selected for their attractive appearance, but the term does not imply anything about their qualities, physically.

*Engineering:* strong dense bricks used for high load-bearing walls, water retaining structures and acid resistant work. They are made to two classifications – (a) crushing strength not less than 69 mn/m$^2$ and a water absorption of not more than 4.5 per cent and (b) crushing strength of not less than 48.5 mn/m$^2$ and a water absorption of not more than 7 per cent.

## Brick qualities

*Interior quality:* not suitable for exterior use.

*Ordinary quality:* these bricks are durable for all normal

purposes, but need to be protected by correct detailing when used in severely exposed parts of a structure such as the tops of walls, retaining walls which do not have a waterproof backing and parapet walls.

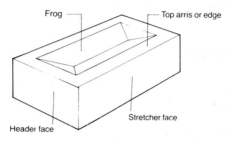

Frog — Top arris or edge

Stretcher face

Header face

*Fig. 20. Pressed brick with frog*

*Special quality:* these are durable bricks which can be used in the most exposed conditions where the brickwork may become saturated and frozen in winter.

Common and facing bricks may be offered in all three qualities, but in practice, all engineering bricks are frost resistant.

It is common to call all bricks solid even though they may contain holes or frogs (shallow indents in the bed face of the brick), Figs. 20 and 21, because these have little bearing on the performance of the brick, although they do dictate the way it is laid; frogs are laid downward and bricks

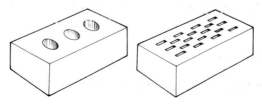

*Fig. 21. Two types of perforated wirecut bricks*

with holes can only be laid on their edges when used for paving.

## Calcium sillicate bricks

Loadbearing, common and facing bricks made from calcium sillicate (also called sand lime) are made in six classes defined in British Standard 187:1978 from the strongest,

*Fig. 22. Processes involved in clay brick manufacture*

Class 7 down to Class 2. As a general guide a minimum of Class 4 is required for retaining walls, sills and copings. A minimum of Class 3 for parapets and free-standing external walls. Class 2 is suitable for general walling above 150 mm above ground level. As with clay bricks, specific guidance should be sought from the maker or supplier where there is any doubt as to suitability.

## Brick sizes

The British Standard brick is $215 \times 102.5 \times 65$ mm. When a 10 mm mortar joint has been allowed for the size is

$225 \times 112.5 \times 75$ mm. This means that you would need 60 bricks per square metre for a wall half-brick (102.5 mm) thick built in stretcher bond. Of course, if the wall was one-brick (215 mm) thick you would need twice as many bricks. This does not include wastage.

Cut bricks are needed to help form the various bonds in brickwork, and are used in the following standard sizes: ¼ bat; ½ bat; ¾ bat; Queen closer, King closer and split – see Fig. 23.

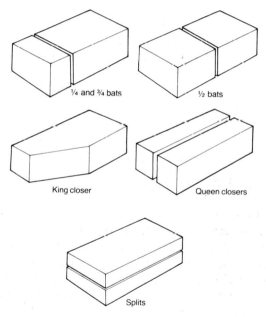

*Fig. 23. Standard cut bricks*

Purpose-made special bricks are available in many shapes to suit all types of construction. One common type of special is the squint which is used to construct corners out of square; 120° and 135° squints are the two standard ones, but other

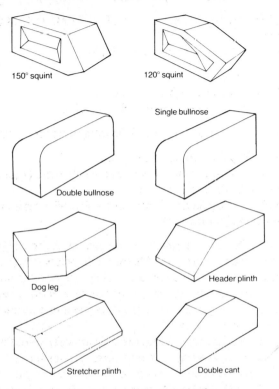

*Fig. 24. Purpose-made special bricks*

angles can be made to order. For an internal angle the dogleg brick is used. Single and double bullnose specials are used to give rounded corners, while plinth bricks reduce the thickness of a wall. Fig. 24 shows some examples of specials.

## Blocks

Concrete and insulating blocks are larger than bricks and are made in many sizes, the minimum standard face area is

$290 \times 215$ mm, with thicknesses of 75, 100, 150, 200 and 225 mm.

There are three main types of blocks:

(A) dense blocks;
(B) lightweight loadbearing blocks;
(C) lightweight non-loadbearing blocks.

Each type is available in the following three specifications:

Solid – less then 20 per cent voids;
Hollow – more than 25 per cent voids with large holes going right through the block;
Cellular – more than 25 per cent voids with holes which do not go right through.

Type A blocks are made from normal dense aggregate concrete, and most are suitable for work below ground level or work exposed to the weather. They are poor insulators against heat loss and the majority are very permeable. The drab appearance means that they are usually concealed by a surface finish or painted.

Type B blocks are manufactured from lightweight aggregates, such as pumice, foamed slag, pulverised fuel ash pellets, expanded clay and cement, or by mixing pulverized fuel ash, cement, and a foaming agent to form a lightweight aerated concrete block. Aerated blocks can be used below ground level but not the denser types. Any work exposed to the weather must be protected by a surface finish.

The insulation properties of type B blocks, combined with their loadbearing properties, make them ideal for the inner skin of a loadbearing external cavity wall. For this application a foam plastic layer is bonded to one side for better external wall insulation and the foam faces into the cavity.

Type C non-loadbearing blocks are generally used in partition work and are suitable for plastering. However, as walls built with them are not very stable during building,

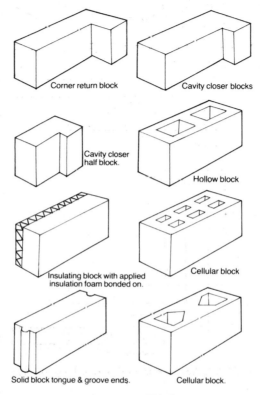

Corner return block

Cavity closer blocks

Cavity closer half block.

Hollow block

Insulating block with applied insulation foam bonded on.

Cellular block

Solid block tongue & groove ends.

Cellular block.

*Fig. 25. Types of block*

they are restrained at the top until the work is completed. Fig. 25 shows examples of block types.

At the corners and ends of walls, cut or purpose-made blocks are needed to provide the bond pattern. In Fig. 26, method 1 shows a half block used to provide the bond from the end of the wall while at the corner another cut block is used to make the thickness of the return block up to $\frac{1}{2}$ a block. In method 2 purpose-made blocks are used at the corner and a $\frac{1}{2}$ block is used at the wall end. Special blocks

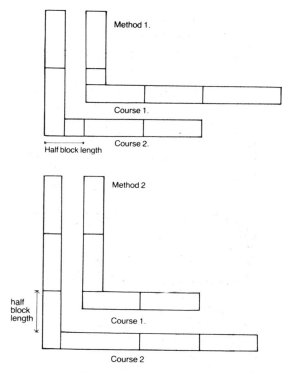

*Fig. 26. Bonding blockwork corners using cut blocks*

are also made for closing the cavity at door and window openings.

Cellular blocks are bedded with the holes down so that the cavities trap a pocket of air; this keeps the weight down and improves the heat insulation.

Hollow blocks have a mortar bed spread along each side. Known as shell bedding, the webs are kept clear (Fig. 27). The cross joints are also applied on both faces leaving the centre of the joint clear. This type of blockwork is often used for agricultural and other buildings which do not have

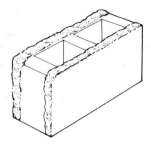

*Fig. 27. Shell bedding of hollow blockwork*

to be of cavity wall construction. They can be used to construct retaining walls by inserting mild steel reinforcement and filling the vertical cavities with concrete (Fig. 28). These walls are also used in agricultural work as linings for silage pits and slurry containers.

Facing blocks are used increasingly for interior work, painted or left plain. It requires care and skill to produce good quality facing work, the joints must be even and the blockwork plumbed and levelled accurately. The blocks

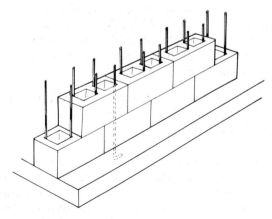

*Fig. 28. Reinforced hollow blockwork*

must be handled carefully so that they are not damaged. Profiled moulds give a rock face or geometric relief pattern. Some blocks are split by a hydraulic guillotine to give a varied face with rough texture. All these types of facing blocks are available in colours by using pigments in the concrete or by using a stone dust facing to the main body of the block. The aggregates used for the split blocks can enhance the appearance and give varied texture to the block face.

Reconstituted stone blocks are made to give the appearance of a particular type of stone by using the stone dust and coloured cement on the face of the main concrete body of the block.

## Mortar

Mortars must have the following properties:

- (A) be workable, and easily used;
- (B) retain water on the mortar board;
- (C) securely bind the bricks together;
- (D) form a weather resistant durable joint;
- (E) be of similar strength to the bricks or blocks;
- (F) easily mixed using locally produced materials for economy.

Materials for mortar are sand as the bulk, with lime or a cement as the binder and hardener, and water which must be clean and drinkable.

*Sand:* a medium fine sand is required. A coarse sand will produce mortar that will not bind together or hold up on the trowel and will not spread easily. A very fine sand needs more cement and water to make it workable and tends to be sticky and, like the coarse type, it does not spread easily.

*Cement:* ordinary Portland cement is mainly used because of its ability to set and harden even in wet conditions, to grip the bricks and blocks and to form a durable weather resistant joint. The setting is a chemical reaction with water which results in a crystal formation.

In addition to Portland cements, masonry cement containing plasticizing agents is available which produces a very good workable brickwork mortar. In areas where the subsoil is aggressive towards ordinary cement, a sulphate resistant cement must be used to resist the sulphates in the soil.

*Lime:* although lime gradually hardens by exposure to the air, it never reaches the strength of cement. White hydrated lime is mainly used as a plasticizer in a cement–lime–sand mix to give workability and water retention to the mortar and it also binds the sand particles together. Blue Lias lime, available in some parts of Britain, is a hydraulic lime which has a setting and hardening action similar to cement, but is not as hard.

**Mortar mixes**

Lime–sand mortars are very rarely used in present-day constructions, instead a cement–lime–sand mortar is used with the lime acting as a plasticizing agent making the mortar workable for the bricklayer and giving properties very suitable for bricks and some lightweight blocks. As straight cement–sand mortars have poor workability and water retention, a chemical plasticizer is usually added to improve these factors. Plasticizers entrain millions of tiny air bubbles in the mix lubricating the cement and sand particles and making them flow easily. The mortar type and strength should be compatible with the bricks or blocks being used.

Ready-mixed lime mortar delivered to site in a special truck can be purchased in most parts of Britain and has to be tipped on a prepared site or into a steel bunker. The mortar is remixed as required with the cement added in the mixer. This mortar is often used where a coloured mortar is required; the colour pigment content is carefully measured by weight giving a more consistent colour than can be mixed on site. A cement–lime–sand mortar mix (1:1:6), chemically retarded to delay setting for up to 60 hours, can be supplied in skip containers or discharged into a steel bunker on site; this does not need remixing, but must be used within two days of delivery. This type of mortar is delivered in large quantities which may not be suitable for small jobs.

Dry ready-mixed cement and sand in 50 kg paper sacks may be a cleaner way of getting material to an upper floor in a building which is occupied, but it is more expensive than purchasing sand and cement separately. It is, however, a useful way of purchasing mortar materials for small jobs.

Mixing mortar by hand with a shovel is suitable for small batches. The materials are measured and placed in a heap which is turned over at least three times making sure that all materials are combined evenly in the dry state. The heap

*Fig. 29. Mixing mortar with a shovel (1)*

*Fig. 30. Mixing mortar with a shovel (2)*

is then opened out with the shovel, Fig. 29, and water is added. The mixing is carried out inside the ring with more water being added as necessary (Fig. 30). Finally, the heap is turned over three times to complete the mixing. If plasticizer is being used it is measured and poured into the mixing water, however it is not possible to gain full value from a plasticizer unless mixing by machine.

Machine mixing produces a better quality mortar and, of course, is easier. Small portable mixers are readily available for hire with petrol, diesel or electric motors. Fig. 31 shows two types of mixer. Larger machines are needed, of course,

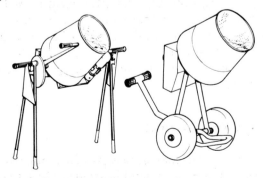

Fig. 31. Small portable concrete or mortar mixers

to keep several bricklayers working. If the machine is started by turning a handle care should be taken to keep the thumb out of the way and not round the handle. Electric mixers must have 110 volt transformed supply for safe working.

## Concrete

Concrete is a mixture of aggregates bound together by cement which hardens into a solid mass. The four materials which make up concrete are:

- (A) coarse aggregate, this consists of natural gravel or crushed rock which does not pass through a 5 mm sieve. This material makes up the bulk of the concrete; it must be clean, have high crushing strength, and well graded from the maximum size to minimum size particles.
- (B) the fine aggregate is natural sand or a fine aggregate of crushed rock which must pass through a 5 mm sieve. Fine aggregate must also be clean and well graded. It fills the void spaces in coarse aggregate. A coarse grain sand is better than fine for concrete.
- (C) generally, ordinary Portland cement is used to bind the materials together and harden the mass.
- (D) water must be of drinking quality. The water hydrates the cement and combines with it to form the crystals, it also lubricates the mix allowing it to be worked into place.

## Batching concrete materials

Measuring the quantities of materials can be done by volume using buckets for small quantities or gauge boxes for larger

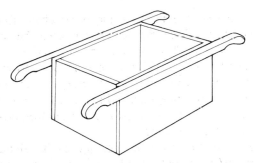

Fig. 32. Gauge box (*bottomless*)

amounts (Fig. 32). The gauge box is equal in size to one bag of cement (1¼ cu ft) and therefore can be used to produce batches relative to one bag of cement. Standard cement–sand-aggregate mix ratios are: 1:1½:3; 1:2:4; 1:2½:5; and 1:3:6. These proportions of aggregates are based on the fact that 40 to 50 per cent of the coarse aggregate is void space which must be filled with fine aggregate if a solid concrete is to result. Batching by volume is not very accurate because sand is affected by bulking which is the change in volume which takes place due to varying moisture content. Allowance can be made for this and a satisfactory concrete mixed, but a better more consistent concrete is produced by weigh-batching. All ready-mixed concrete is batched by weight and consistent, reliable-performance concrete can be obtained every time. The ratio of cement to aggregate has to be such that the finished concrete is strong and durable enough for the work it is expected to do. The ratio of water to cement in the mix is very critical. Some of the water will combine with the cement in the chemical reaction of setting. The rest of the water only makes the mix workable and then after hardening it evaporates, leaving voids behind which weaken the concrete.

It is important that this workability water is kept to the

minimum so that maximum value is obtained from the cement. However, if insufficient water is used the concrete may be too dry for full compaction and again a weaker concrete results. Workability is affected by factors other than water, such as the shape of the aggregate (i.e. rounded gravel is easier to work than cubical crushed rock). The lower aggregate cement ratios are more workable and coarse sand is better than fine sand.

Mixing the concrete has to be thorough so that all particles are covered with cement. Hand mixing with shovels is all right for small quantities, but cannot be as good as machine mixing. The materials are turned and mixed three times in a dry state, then water is added and the concrete mixed with the water and turned over wet three times. Machine mixers turn out very well mixed concrete so long as they are not overloaded and are maintained in a clean condition. Small portable mixers with rotating, tilting drums and driven by petrol or electric motors are easily moved and used (Fig. 31). They can be carried in the boot of a car and wheeled like a barrow by one man. Larger ones are only practical for large volume work. In ideal conditions the mixing should be done next to the placing position, but this is not always possible and the mixed concrete may have to be transported. Wheelbarrows are suitable for short distances. A small dumper truck would be more suitable for longer distances and larger quantities. Moving concrete costs money and does not contribute to the progress of the job, also transporting it over rough terrain tends to unmix or segregate the constituants, therefore, it is good practice to reduce transportation as much as possible. Ready-mixed concrete must be discharged into the working position or as near as possible. Mixing on site should also be as close to placing as possible.

## Laying concrete

Formwork supports the concrete while it is setting and gives the concrete its final shape. It must be strong enough to resist the stress of the wet concrete as it is being compacted. Screws and bolts are much better than nails to keep the formwork in place.

Concrete must be placed in layers not more than 150 mm deep and each layer compacted to make sure that the result is a solid mass. Hand compaction by shovel, podger, or beater is suitable for concrete in beams or trenches, but a tamping beam is needed for a slab (Fig. 33). The object is to shake out all the air and made sure that the finished concrete has no voids.

Surface finishing will be necessary on any concrete which will be exposed in the final work unless a surface finish has been provided by the formwork. Hand trowelling by steel or wood float gives a smooth even surface, but has to be carried out on a surface that has been tamped and screeded to an even level finish. The steel float will close and polish

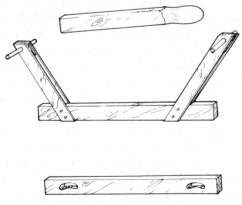

*Fig. 33. Hand tamper and tamping beams*

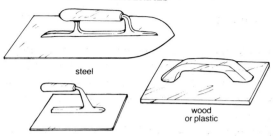

*Fig. 34. Hand floats*

the surface and give a very smooth finish. The wood float gives a slightly textured finish (Fig. 34). Any surface finish treatment can only be applied on concrete when it has begun to set, it is impossible to surface finish wet concrete. This is another good reason for keeping the water cement ratio as low as possible. Other surface finishes can be applied by brush or by washing and lightly brushing the surface cement away exposing the aggregates.

When the concrete has been surface-finished it must be covered for at least 14 days to protect it from rain, sun and wind while it is setting. This curing ensures that the concrete does not dry out before hardening and is very important if the concrete is going to gain all the potential strength of the cement. Curing means keeping the moisture in the concrete. This can be done by using a patent surface sealer, covering the concrete with wet sacks, flooding it with water, sprinkling it with wet sand which is kept wet or covering it with polythene sheets pressed on to the surface. Rapid drying will give a dusty surface possibly with shrinkage cracks that will wear quickly. Newly-laid concrete must be protected from frost as it will disrupt the mix and break up the concrete. If frost is a possibility, insulation of some kind must be used to prevent the concrete being affected. This protection can be achieved by putting polythene sheeting over the damp concrete then placing insulation such as hessian or empty cement bags with straw inside, or some similar covering, over the surface.

Concrete materials are obtained from two main sources:

(A) direct ordering from suppliers and manufacturers is suitable for large bulk deliveries. Generally, they will only deliver full lorry loads which may be too much for small jobs or need too much unloading and storage space.

(B) a builder's merchant carries stocks of most items and can supply small quantities immediately in most cases. The materials and components can be seen and if not in stock the merchant probably has samples. A builder's merchant will also order and arrange delivery of larger quantities direct from the manufacturer.

Some materials are packed in 50 kg plastic or paper sacks depending on whether they are wet or dry. Sand, gravel and stone chippings are obtainable in plastic sacks while cement, lime and plaster are packed in paper. Waterproof storage must be provided on site for the three latter. Moisture penetration of the bags will rapidly cause deterioration of these materials. Bricks and blocks are packed on pallets or in bound packs with polythene shrink wrapping for weather protection. The off-loading crane for these packs is fixed to the delivery lorry, the driver operator can unload and stack packs on site without assistance, but to be economical in use these lorries need to carry about 5000 bricks. Sand, gravel and aggregates are delivered in bulk from the pits, quarries or rail depots, in tipper lorries either by weight (tonnes) or volume (cubic metres), usually loads of 10 tonnes or 10 cubic metres are the minimum. Bulk delivery of cement for site storage in silos is by road tanker carrying 20 tonnes or more. Concrete ready mixed is delivered to site in mixer truck loads of five or six cubic metres. The hire of the truck mixer and the cost of the concrete is taken separately so smaller loads can be obtained, but the full cost of the truck must be paid. A similar cost applies to ready-mixed mortar for site delivery.

# 3

# Building the walls

**Bonding**

The arrangement of bricks to a definite pattern in a wall is called bonding. The bricks are overlapped so that the vertical joints do not form a continuous straight line through the thickness or along the courses. This distributes any imposed loads throughout the wall and avoids cracking (Fig. 35).

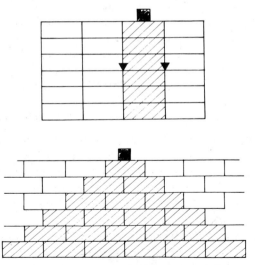

*Fig. 35. Showing the effect of a load on an unbonded and a bonded wall*

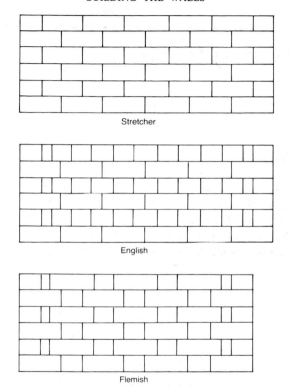

*Fig. 36. Face appearance of Stretcher bond, English bond and Flemish bond*

Stretcher bond is the simplest as the bricks are placed lengthwise along the wall overlapping half way over each other and producing a wall 112.5 mm or half-brick thick.

The bond is achieved by starting alternate courses with a half brick (Fig. 36). At corners the half brick is provided by the return brick.

In housing all external walls are built with two half-brick walls in stretcher bond separated by a cavity, but attached to each other by wall ties.

Solid walls one brick thick are built in either English

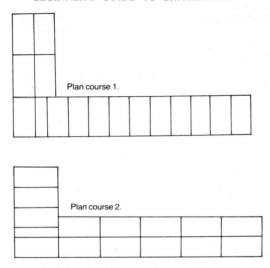

*Fig. 37. English bond return one brick thick*

bond or Flemish bond. English bond consists of a course of stretchers (bricks laid along the wall) and a course of headers (bricks laid endways through the thickness of the wall). In order to provide the bond pattern it is necessary to lay a queen closer (see Fig. 23) after the first header (Figs. 36 and 37). This is considered to be the strongest bond because there are no vertical joints running straight up through the wall.

Flemish bond is considered to be more decorative if a little weaker because in certain places a vertical joint runs right up through the wall, although of course it is not visible from the outside. This bond consists of alternate headers and stretchers in each course. Again the bond is created by laying a queen closer after the first header in those courses which start with a header.

Figs. 36 to 40 show the bonding arrangements for walls

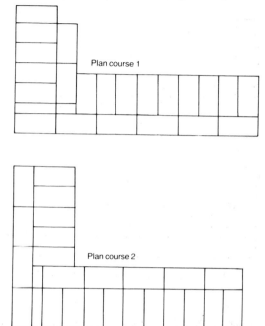

*Fig. 38. English bond return one and a half bricks thick*

of one brick and one and a half bricks thick in English and Flemish bonds.

To carry out brick or blocklaying effectively and with economy of effort, bricks and blocks should be stacked at intervals along the wall, alternating with a mortar spot board, and set back from the wall line 600 mm to allow space for working. Brick stacks should be set on firm and level ground to avoid the stack falling over. A brick on edge or a block is placed under each corner of the spot board to reduce the bending effort required to pick up mortar. The materials must be positioned with the openings in the wall in mind.

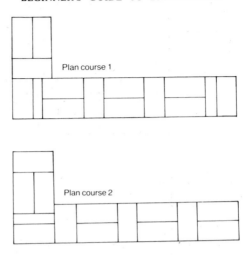

*Fig. 39. Flemish bond return one brick thick*

The first stage when building a wall is to build up the corners or stop ends. It is essential to spread an even bed of mortar right up to the corner or end and to ensure that the bricks are level and plumb. The corner bricks must be pressed down as accurately as possible into the mortar and then checked for plumb and tested with the gauge (Fig. 41). Each course must be levelled then ranged with the level for face plane alignment (Fig. 42). The beginner will find this the most difficult part of bricklaying and will need to take care and to check every course before laying the next. Accurate corners are essential to make sure that the wall aligns correctly. They are built to about 600 to 900 mm high before filling in the middle part of the wall.

When the corners and ends have been built a line is fixed by inserting the pins in the crossjoint (Figs. 43a and b). The line is stretched as tight as possible and set accurately along the top arris or edge of the course. Where a long wall is being built, the line is likely to sag and has to be supported

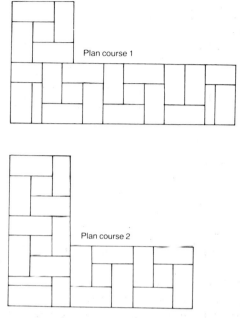

*Fig. 40. Flemish bond return one and a half bricks thick*

in the middle or in some cases may need more than one support. This is done by bedding a brick in position plumb and to the gauge mark, fitting the tingleplate (Fig. 44) on the line, then placing on the brick and weighted with another brick (Fig. 45). To prevent pinholes or line marks in newly pointed corners, corner blocks (Fig. 46) can be used to hold the line in position. Tingles may have to be used on a short line on a windy day to prevent it from blowing about. The tingle can also be set to correct level by eyesight, sighting through from one end to the other (Fig. 45).

*Stopped end:* this is a plumb end which is not a corner or return.

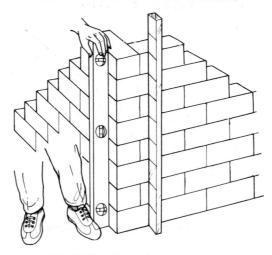

*Fig. 41. Plumbing and gauging a corner*

*Racking back and toothing:* these are methods of leaving work which is to be continued at a later date (Figs. 47 and 48). A toothing is more difficult to work into and must be carefully built to ensure full joints or the joint will not be very strong.

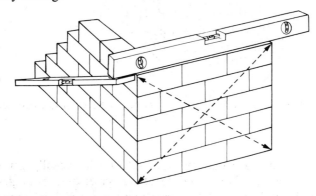

*Fig. 42. Levelling and checking faceplane on a corner and short return*

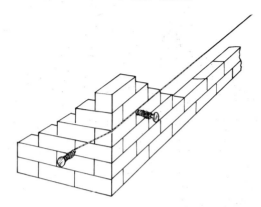

*Fig. 43a. Alternative positions for line pins*

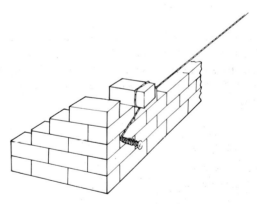

*Fig. 43b. Line fixed by brick when near the top of the corner to prevent the top bricks being pulled off*

*Indents:* these are pockets built into a wall usually three courses high to allow a wall to be connected at right angles (Fig. 49). Indents are left every three courses high in brickwork and every other course in blockwork.

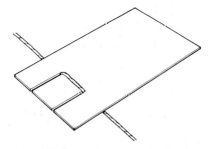

*Fig. 44. Sheet metal tingle plate fitted on the line*

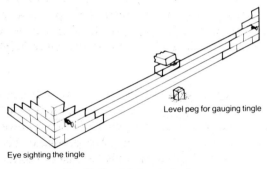

Level peg for gauging tingle

Eye sighting the tingle

*Fig. 45. Eyesighting tingle plate*

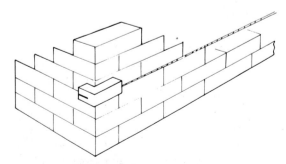

*Fig. 46. Corner block in position*

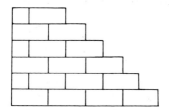

*Fig. 47. Stop end and racking back*

*Gauge staff:* this is used to ensure that courses are kept to a uniform height and that the walling is built level. A level peg is set at the required position usually at corners at the damp-proof course (d.p.c.) level. Alternatively, a nail can be set into a bedjoint or under the d.p.c. and projected to hold the gauge. Other useful heights can be indicated on the gauge staff, such as cill height, lintel height, floor level, etc.

*Cutting concrete blocks:* concrete blocks can be cut by hand using a club hammer and bolster chisel, but a better way to avoid less waste is by using a petrol or electric power-driven abrasive cutting disc, or a hydraulic guillotine. The cutting disc does a good job but can only be used outdoors because of the dust created and, with a petrol-driven machine, the motor fumes.

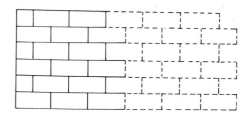

*Fig. 48. Stop end and toothing*

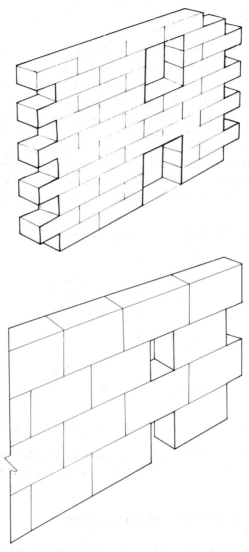

*Fig. 49. Indents in brickwork and blockwork*

## Wall stability

Brickwalls and blockwalls over 100 mm thick are fairly stable during construction and can be built up to scaffold height quite safely, although strong winds can blow a half brick wall over if it is not part of a complete structure. Blockwork 75 mm or 100 mm thick is not very stable when being built as an isolated wall. To improve their stability profiles are set up and used to assist in keeping the walls plumb. The wood profiles 75 mm × 50 mm section are plumbed and wedged in position at wall ends, inside corners or in the centre of walls more than 4 metres long (Fig. 50).

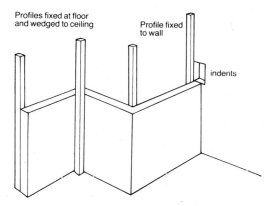

Profiles fixed at floor and wedged to ceiling

Profile fixed to wall

indents

*Fig. 50. Use of temporary profiles to support new blockwork*

An alternative method is to build only four or five courses of blocks and let this work set before raising the wall higher.

## Effects of the weather on brick and blockwork

Before use, bricks and blocks must be kept dry on site by covering them with tarpaulin or polythene sheet; some types will be delivered in polythene protected packs. It is impossible to build with wet bricks and blocks as the mortar will run and plumbing is impractical. Wet blockwork will suffer shrinkage cracking when it dries out. Protection of work which is not intended to be exposed to the weather (such as lightweight internal partition blockwork), is necessary if it is built before the roof is complete. If rain starts while work is proceeding then the walls and the brick or block stacks must be covered. When working on a scaffold, turn up the inside board to prevent rain splashing from the board and staining the face of the wall. In hot sunny weather some very absorbent walling materials may be improved by damping before use but this is not recommended for most blocks or for concrete and sandlime bricks.

When working in cold weather check the temperature with a thermometer. If the temperature is falling towards freezing then work must stop and covers must be put on the walling before the freezing point is reached. If the temperature is rising, perhaps after an overnight frost, wait until it is at least 2°C and rising before starting to lay bricks. Cold weather conditions slow down the hardening of the cement in mortar or concrete and below freezing point the water in the mix turns to ice, expands, and disrupts the walling or concrete.

Admixtures can be used to prevent the mortar or concrete from freezing, most of them work by accelerating the setting time and increasing the heat generated by the setting reaction. The work still has to be covered for protection and to contain the heat, and all aggregate materials have to be protected from freezing. The small amount of mortar in a wall does not generate much heat and certainly the admix does not keep the bricklayer warm.

# 4

# **Work below d.p.c.**

**Setting out equipment**

1. Tape measure, steel or plastic
2. Straightedge
3. Spirit level
4. Wood square
5. Lines
6. Nails
7. Pegs
8. Profile board
9. Hammer

**Setting out a small building**

The position of a building is fixed by relating it to an existing feature near the site. If the building is to be set out in relation to a road then the front will have to be on or behind the building line. This line is established by the local authority planning department who will take into account future possible road works, visibility for traffic and the position and line of other buildings nearby. The line may be given as a distance from the crown of the road or possibly a line taken between the frontages of two existing buildings. If the proposed building is not situated near a road or existing buildings then the frontage line may have to

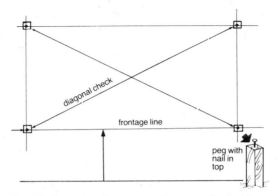

*Fig. 51. Setting out the corners of a rectangular building*

be fixed by measurement from a hedge, wall or similar feature.

The first stage is to set out the frontage line of the building by stretching a line tightly between two pegs. Position one end and drive in a peg (with a nail in the top) to fix the exact corner spot (Fig. 51). The other front corner is then measured and a peg driven with a nail in the top. Next, the back left-hand corner peg position is measured and squared from the frontage line. Then the back right-hand corner peg position is measured and this peg is driven firmly into the ground and the nail set into it. The setting out can now be checked for accuracy by measuring the diagonals which should be exactly the same.

Profile boards on which the positions of the trench, concrete foundations and the brick walls will be marked are set up at sufficient distance from the corners so that they will not interfere with the digging of the trenches or be damaged or moved by a mechanical digger (Fig. 52). Profiles consist of a board supported on stout pegs. On the top edge of the board is marked the face of the brickwork using the frontage line and pegs already set up. From these marks the width of the concrete and the width of the trench, if it is to be

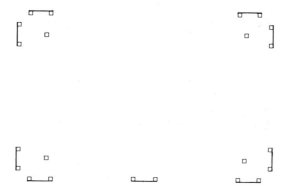

*Fig. 52. Profiles fixed at corners*

wider than the concrete, are measured and marked (Fig. 53).
These marks are then made permanent by cutting them into
the wood with a saw, or by nails.

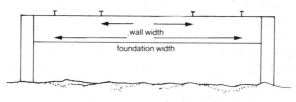

*Fig. 53. Profile*

From these main setting out points, the intermediate walls
and any projecting parts of the building are measured and
marked on their own profile boards (Fig. 54).

For small buildings such as a garage, a wooden square
can be used for the setting out (Fig. 55), or the 3:4:5 method
can be used (Fig. 56). Small houses and bungalows can be
squared by calculating the diagonal length and using two
tapes (Fig. 57). To complete the setting out a level peg or
datum peg will be needed at each corner. These pegs are
levelled at d.p.c. position by using a straightedge and spirit
level (Fig. 58), or an optical level such as the Cowley auto-

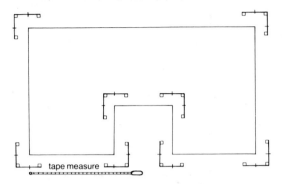

*Fig. 54. Measuring intermediate profiles*

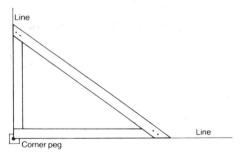

*Fig. 55. Squaring the setting out lines*

matic (Fig. 59). String lines are fixed to the outer nails in the profiles and the lines of the trenches marked by using a shovel or by a line of sand on the ground. If the excavation is done by hand on a very small job there should be no possibility of disturbing the profiles and datum pegs, but if by machine it is essential to set the profiles well back from the excavation to allow room for the machine to work (Fig. 60).

The depth of the trench is determined by taking a level from a datum peg using a straightedge and spirit level, then

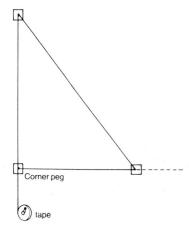

*Fig. 56. The 3:4:5 method of setting out*

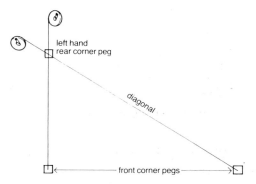

*Fig. 57. Setting out using two tapes and calculated diagonal*

using a gauge lath to set a peg at the level required for the foundation concrete. This will ensure that the foundation brickwork or blockwork will properly course in up to d.p.c. level (Fig. 61). As the trench is excavated further pegs are levelled off from the first one. The accuracy can be checked by gauging down from one of the other corner datum pegs.

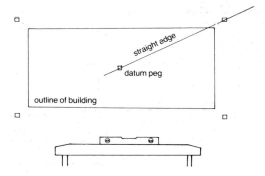

*Fig. 58. Corner level pegs, straightedge and spirit level*

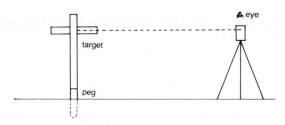

*Fig. 59. Optical level*

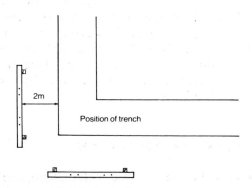

*Fig. 60. Profiles set back from corners to allow room for machine digging*

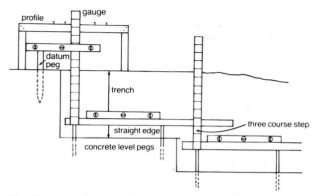

*Fig. 61. Gauging down to obtain correct height of concrete level pegs*

The profiles are used again when lining and setting out the foundation walls.

### Squaring using the 3:4:5 method (Fig. 56)

The tape end ring is hooked over the nail in the corner peg A. From here 3 m is measured along the frontage line and peg B is driven with a nail. The tape is turned round this nail and stretched out tight. The tape is then let out to 12 m mark and held against the nail in peg A. Peg C is driven with a nail in the top at 8 m. A plastic-coated tape is required for this operation as a steel one will not bend round the nails. The measurements do not have to be in metres but have to be in the ratio of 3:4:5.

### Foundations and work up to d.p.c. level

Building regulations require that all foundations will safely carry the combined loads of the building and resist any

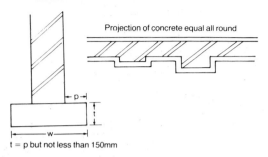

Fig. 62. *Thickness of foundation and projection of foundation concrete*

settlement that could cause damage and be deep enough to be unaffected by weather conditions. This is ensured in most domestic and small buildings by constructing a strip concrete foundation. The concrete must be mixed not less than 1 bag of cement to $0.1\,m^3$ fine and $0.2\,m^3$ coarse aggregate. The width of concrete is specified in the regulations for various loadings and types of soil. Thickness must be not less than 150 mm. If the spread either side of the wall is greater than 150 mm then the thickness must be increased to equal it (Fig. 62). Where there are any projections on the walls then there must be equal projections on the concrete foundation. Depth below ground level must be at least 600 mm.

If the site is sloping the concrete will have to be stepped. Steps must be equal to courses of bricks or blocks. The higher level slab must overlap the lower level by a minimum of 300 mm (Fig. 63). The concrete must be well tamped to

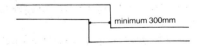

Fig. 63. *Overlapping of stepped concrete foundations*

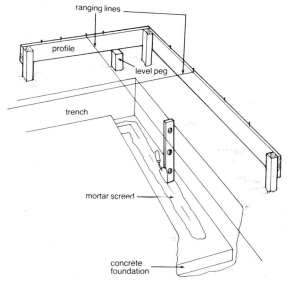

*Fig. 64. Marking out the position of the walling on the concrete foundation*

the level of the pegs set in the trench bottom. If the foundation is stepped start at the lowest level, working upwards.

When the concrete has hardened the ranging lines are fixed to the profiles to give the wall positions. These have to be plumbed down and marked on to the concrete foundation so that the brickwork can be set out correctly. The spirit level is held plumb against the ranging line, using a stick to steady it. A line is marked with the trowel point on a very thin screed of mortar smoothed on to the concrete (Fig. 64). Four of these marks are needed at each corner. The brickwork is built up at each corner to the d.p.c. level, racking the courses back and checking for accuracy with the ranging lines at each course.

When the corners are complete, the wall between can be built. In a stepped foundation count the courses down from

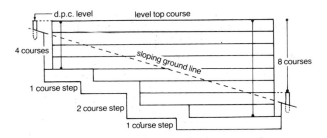

*Fig. 65. Stepped foundation and wall below d.p.c. level*

d.p.c. level when fixing the line to make sure that the wall
will course properly (Fig. 65). A section of typical foundation and work up to d.p.c. for a small building with
solid concrete floor is shown in Fig. 66. An example of the
underbuilding associated with a suspended timber floor is
shown in Fig. 67. These floors are more expensive than solid
concrete unless the building is on a steeply sloping site and
a lot of underbuilding is required to make up the level.

Air vents must be built-in above ground level with a
purpose-made duct to take the air through the cavity. The
air bricks are terra cotta, concrete or brick with louvre
openings or small square openings. The air bricks must let
air flow through, but prevent mice or similar small animals
getting into the foundation. It is essential to make sure that

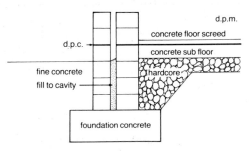

*Fig. 66. Section through foundation wall and solid floor*

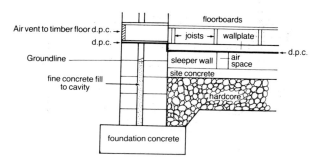

*Fig. 67. Section through foundation wall and hollow timber floor*

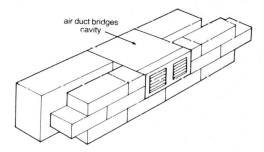

*Fig. 68. Air vent through external wall*

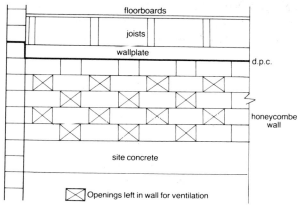

*Fig. 69. Honeycombe sleeper wall*

the ventilator is at least 150 mm above ground level to prevent any possibility of the soil building up in front and blocking the airway.

An air duct through the cavity can be built with four pieces of slate instead of a purpose-made sleeve (Fig. 68); this prevents the air going into the wall cavity. To allow the free flow of air under the floor the walls must be built in a honeycombe pattern (Fig. 69). This applies to the foundations of partition walls as well as the sleeper walls which support the ground floor joists.

# 5

---

# **Scaffolding**

An important part of the equipment for bricklaying is the scaffolding necessary to enable the bricklayer to carry out his work. The scaffold has to be wide enough and strong enough to carry the materials and tools as well as the workman, and the means of access must be safe and secure. Accidents involving falls from scaffolds and ladders are the most common in the building industry and among d.i.y. enthusiasts. The Construction Regulations Working Places are designed to prevent such accidents and if all the regulations were strictly observed then very few of these accidents would take place.

There are many different types of scaffolding available to suit all types of jobs and it may be advisable to obtain advice from a scaffold hire firm if the job is not a straightforward one.

### Trestle scaffolds

The trestles can be made from timber (Fig. 70) or steel (Fig. 71). Steel trestles have the advantage that they fold flat but they are heavier. Never prop up trestles on loose bricks, their legs must always be placed on firm ground. Trestles must be set not more than 2 m apart with planks 37 mm thick, but can be up to 3 m apart with planks 50 mm thick. The scaffold is loaded so that the heaviest loads, usually the

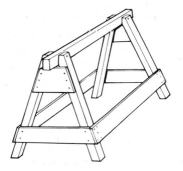

*Fig. 70. Timber trestle*

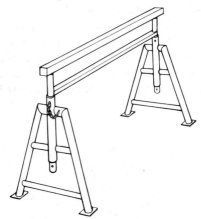

*Fig. 71. Steel trestle*

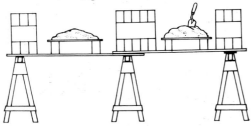

*Fig. 72. A loaded trestle scaffold ready for working*

bricks or blocks, are stacked over or as near to the trestles as possible (Fig. 72). Where a series of trestles is needed because of the length of the work, the planks will have to be lapped. The planks are 225 mm wide and must be bound at the ends with a galvanized steel strap to prevent the wood splitting. Three planks are needed for the materials and two for standing on when working. Timber trestles are 1 m high but the steel ones are adjustable for height from 1 to 1.6 m. Although trestles can be used in two tiers this is not to be recommended as it is not very stable, also the regulations require a handrail and toeboard to be fixed to any scaffold working platform where it is possible to fall 2 m or more. Steel scaffolding built up from tubes and various types of clips is versatile, but does need skill and practice to be able to erect it successfully. A putlog type scaffold built from tubing and clips is shown in Fig. 73. The toeboard is fixed to prevent tools, bricks, etc., being kicked or knocked off

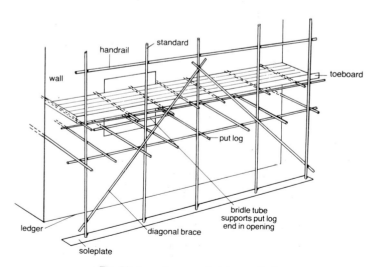

*Fig. 73. Line diagram of putlog scaffold*

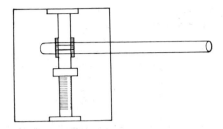

*Fig. 74a. Tying a scaffold to a reveal screwjack fixed into an opening*

during working. The handrail must be fixed at a height of
1 m above the working platform. There are numerous steel
scaffolding systems which consist of prefabricated frames
and sections which can be slotted together easily and provide
a rigid safe working platform with a minimum of effort.
Putlog type scaffolds are dependent on the wall for stability.
Other types of scaffolding are called independant because
they are freestanding, but in both cases stability must be
provided by tying the scaffold into the wall. Two methods
are shown in Figs. 74a and b.

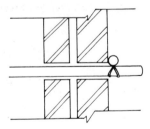

*Fig. 74b. Tying a scaffold by taking a tube through the wall and fixing a cross
tube behind the wall*

A ladder must be used for gaining access to the working
platform. Regulations stipulate that wooden ladders should
not be painted to ensure that the true condition of the wood
can be seen. The ladder must be fixed at the top and project

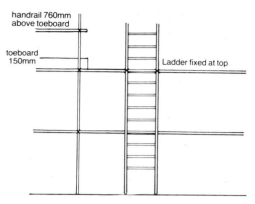

handrail 760mm
above toeboard

toeboard
150mm

Ladder fixed at top

*Fig. 75. Fixing a ladder*

1.066 m above the platform (Figs. 75 and 76) to provide a safe handhold when getting on and off the platform. An angle of 75° is ideal for the ladder, and this is achieved by using a ratio of 1 out to 4 up as shown in Fig. 76.

Many people take short cuts when using scaffolding as it does not form part of the completed work, but a poorly built inadequate scaffold is dangerous to work on and makes

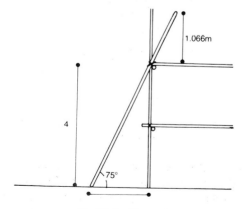

1.066m

4

75°

*Fig. 76. Ladder angle*

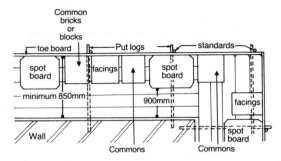

*Fig. 77. Plan of a scaffold loaded ready for use*

the work difficult, adding to the time taken. If the scaffolding is standing in an area where people are passing, warning notices must be posted and flashing lights placed on the scaffold at night.

The scaffold must be loaded to concentrate the greatest loads over the standards. Fig. 77 shows the bricks and mortar set out to suit the bricklayer and also the construction of the scaffolding. Fig. 78 shows the mortar spot board set up on bricks to reduce bending when picking up mortar.

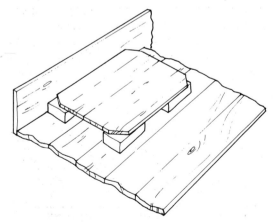

*Fig. 78. Mortar spot board raised on bricks or blocks on a scaffold platform*

# 6

# External walls

Because all bricks and blocks used in walling are porous and permeable solid external walls will always be damp on the inside unless they are very thick. The cavity wall consisting of two skins of brickwork separated by a cavity was introduced early in this century to ensure that the internal walls of a building will remain dry. Additional advantages are that the cavity provides improved heat insulation and the two separate skins can be of entirely different materials, not normally compatible when built together. Building regulations require the wall to be constructed in such a way that the cavity is kept clean, the two skins tied together with metal wall ties to prevent them moving apart and separated by impervious d.p.c. where the cavity is closed.

The wall ties must be rust-proofed, galvanized or stainless-steel wire or twisted steel (Fig. 79). The spacing and distribution are given in the regulations as 900 mm horizontal

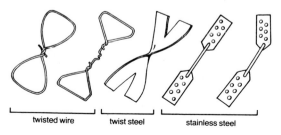

twisted wire     twist steel     stainless steel

*Fig. 79. Wall ties*

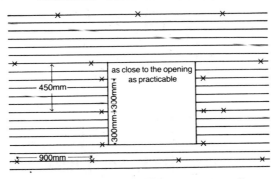

*Fig. 80. Positioning of wall ties in a cavity wall*

and 450 mm vertical with extra ties at angles and alongside
jambs of openings (Fig. 80). Wall ties are kept clean and free
of mortar droppings by using a cavity batten which is drawn
up the cavity and cleaned off at each wall tie level as the work
proceeds (Fig. 81). The jambs of openings are constructed so
that the end of the cavity is closed and a vertical d.p.c. is

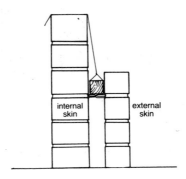

*Fig. 81. A cavity batten in position on the wall tie*

built in to prevent moisture penetration (Fig. 82). This d.p.c.
must start down below the sill d.p.c. or threshold and project
above the opening behind the head d.p.c. To assist in

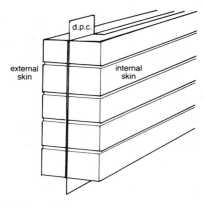

*Fig. 82. Vertical d.p.c. to a closed jamb to an opening*

cleaning the cavity, coring holes are left over the heads of openings and built up after the work is finished (Fig. 83).

At eaves level the cavity has to be closed. If a concrete slab is used to form the soffit of the eaves it must be bedded

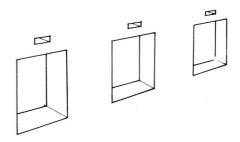

*Fig. 83. Coring holes above window openings in a cavity wall*

on both skins of the wall. It can, however, form a cold bridge across the cavity wall. A course of bricks or blocks laid flat will close the cavity and support the wallplate. This will be protected from the weather by the overhanging eaves of the roof. The wall plate is bedded in place and fixed down

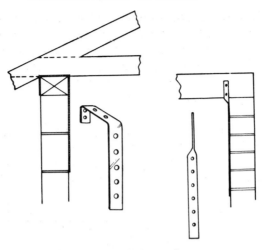

Fig. 84. Wall plate anchors

with brackets at 1 m intervals. These anchor the roof to the walls and prevent it lifting in gales (Fig. 84).

## Openings in walls

An arch or lintel is used to carry the load above an opening and transmit it to the walls. Lintels have the advantage that they present a flat soffit which suits modern architectural styles and allows windows and doors to have flat horizontal heads which are cheaper than the curved heads needed when arches are used. Lintels can be made from timber, natural stone, concrete, steel and brick.

*Timber lintels:* these are rarely used nowadays except for some non-loadbearing partitions, but are often found when renovating old property. Pieces of oak from broken up wooden ships were commonly used for lintels as well as for other building applications.

*Natural stone lintels:* although extensively used in older buildings, stone lintels are now only used for their aesthetic appearance. The length of stone which could be obtained was limited by natural faults in many quarries and so large spans were often impossible and windows had to have mullions to support the shorter lintels.

*Concrete lintels:* concrete lintels are usually reinforced with mild-steel bars. Their advantages compared with timber lintels are fire resistant and rot proof. Also they can be cast to different shapes and lengths with little difficulty (Fig. 85).

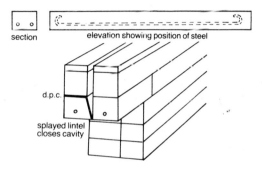

*Fig. 85. Reinforced concrete lintels*

*Steel lintels:* galvanized or corrosion-treated steel lintels can be obtained in several lengths and types to suit most applications. Compared with concrete lintels, they are lighter in weight and therefore easier to fix. Also, they do not require a d.p.c. over the top and offer better heat insulation than concrete ones (Fig. 86a and b).

*Brick lintels:* these lintels are also called soldier arches and are featured in many buildings. They are self-supporting up to a span of 300 mm, but mainly rely on support by either a concrete-backing lintel or a steel-support lintel (Fig. 87).

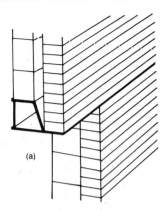

*Fig. 86a. Box-type steel lintel*

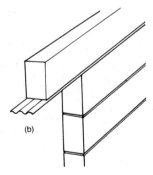

*Fig. 86b. Corrugated lightweight steel lintel for internal block walls*

To ensure the solid jointing necessary joints are often grouted in through a joggle (Fig. 88).

## Fixing frames

Door and window frames can be set up and built-in as work proceeds, or fixed into an opening when the walling is completed. When built-in, the frames must be positioned,

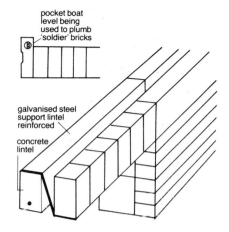

pocket boat
level being
used to plumb
'soldier' bricks

galvanised steel
support lintel
reinforced

concrete
lintel

*Fig. 87. Example of a brick on end lintel*

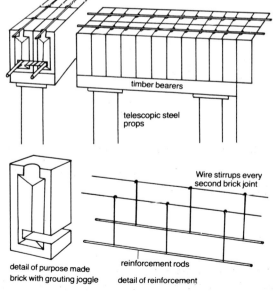

timber bearers

telescopic steel
props

Wire stirrups every
second brick joint

detail of purpose made
brick with grouting joggle

reinforcement rods

detail of reinforcement

*Fig. 88. Details of a reinforced brick lintel*

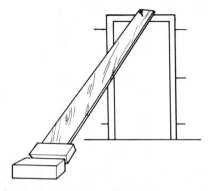

*Fig. 89. Setting up a door frame to be built in*

plumbed and strutted to hold them firm (Fig. 89). Frame cramps are screwed to the back of the frame and built into the bed joints as work proceeds (Fig. 90). Wooden pallettes or pads are built into the brickwork and after the work has set and hardened, nails are driven through the frame into the pad to fix it. Hardwood frames which have to be varnished, and aluminium and plastic frames should not be built in as work proceeds, but are fixed afterwards. A profile frame is set in the opening position to ensure the correct size

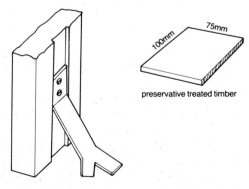

preservative treated timber

*Fig. 90. Metal fixing cramp and wood fixing pad*

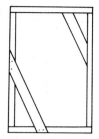

*Fig. 91. Profile frame*

and that the frame will fit properly (Fig. 91). The front edge of the frame is set in line with the vertical d.p.c. Later, a mastic joint can be made between the frame and the d.p.c.

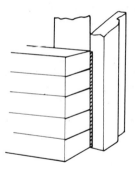

*Fig. 92. Mastic jointing between frame and vertical d.p.c.*

which will prevent water penetration down the side of the frame (Fig. 92).

Internal frames and door linings in plastered walls are wider than the block or brickwork to allow for the thickness of plaster. If these frames are set in position to be built-in, they will project in front of the wall and prevent the use of a line. They must therefore be set back so that they are in line with the wall and are moved forward into the correct position for fixing (Fig. 93).

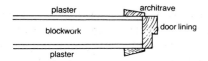

*Fig. 93. Door lining to an internal partition*

## Arches

Arches are a very old method of spanning openings, but mainly used now as a decorative rather than a functional feature. They take many shapes, but are based on the Roman semi-circular arch. The arch can be built with any ordinary bricks in half brick rings using wedge-shaped joints to get round the curve – this is known as a rough ring arch (Fig. 94). To produce a better looking arch the bricks are cut to a taper and used with parallel joints. Purpose-made bricks will give a very neat accurate appearance and allow the use of fine joints such as are used in gauged brickwork. The arch is built over a wooden formwork or centre set up as shown

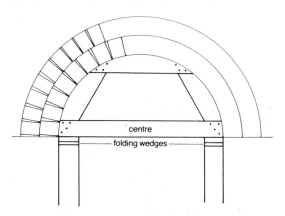

*Fig. 94. Rough ring semicircular arch with arch centre*

in Fig. 94. The use of folding wedges or adjustable props is necessary to allow for removing the centre after the mortar has set and hardened. The arch should be built up from either side towards the crown and jointed to allow for the keybrick to be inserted so that the arch is secure. A line across the front will keep the arch plumb on the face and in line with the wall.

The semi-circular arch is easily set out, all bricks radiating from the centre of the circle. The loads on the arch are transmitted vertically to the supporting wall which makes this arch suitable for building on piers in garden work.

The segmental arch is based on a segment of a circle as shown in Figs. 95a and b. This arch transmits the load on to the abutment skewbacks at an angle and can be built with

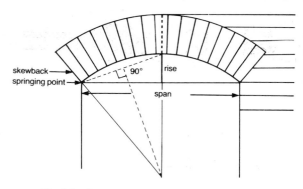

*Fig. 95a. Segmental gauged arch one brick on face*

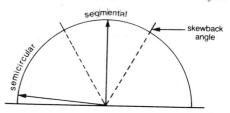

*Fig. 95b. Setting out detail of segmental and semicircular arches*

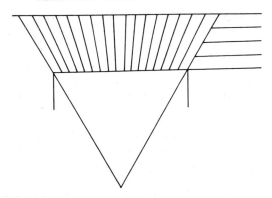

*Fig. 96. A camber arch*

ordinary uncut bricks. A flat or camber arch gives a flat soffit and requires purpose-made bricks as it cannot be cut from ordinary bricks. The camber arch is set out as shown in Fig. 96. It is built across a support which gives a slight camber to the middle 5 mm in 1 m in order to prevent the optical illusion that it is sagging in the middle, which would be the case if it was built flat.

If the bricks for an arch are to be cut, a templet must be prepared for marking them. A full-size outline of the arch is needed and a maximum size brick is drawn. The templet, made from plywood or hardboard, is then traversed around the arch outline to make sure it will work accurately (Fig. 97). The templet may have to be adjusted by shaving

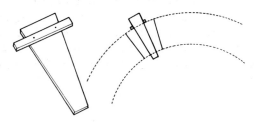

*Fig. 97. A voussoir cutting templet being transversed to prove its shape*

it down or adjusting the thickness of the mortar joint. The bricks are then marked and cut with a club hammer and bolster chisel and finished with a comb hammer.

Arch building was reintroduced into Britain by refugees from religious wars in Holland and Belgium and the following terms associated with arch building remain in use from this time:

Voussoirs – the bricks which make up the arch;
Intrados – the inner line of the arch;
Extrados – the outer line of the arch.

Fig. 98 shows sketches of a built-up arch centre and a turning piece cut out of solid wood; plywood is often used

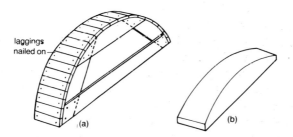

laggings nailed on

(a)

(b)

*Fig. 98.* (left) *Built-up arch centre.* (right) *Turning piece*

in building centres. It must be remembered that the centre has to be removed after the arch has set and may have swelled up by absorbing moisture from the mortar joints or from rainfall. To ensure easy removal, the centre is supported by folding wedges on wood props or by adjustable steel props. The centre should be made a few millimetres under size so that when the props are eased the centre will drop out.

## Cavity insulation batts

These are slabs of insulation material built into the cavity. Mineral wool fibre, expanded polystyrene and glass fibre are the main ones. They are held at each wall tie level by means of plastic disc clips fixed to the wall ties. These clips fix the batts to the inside skin of the wall keeping the cavity clear (Fig. 99).

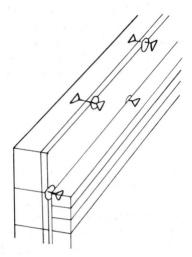

*Fig. 99. Cavity insulation batts in position*

Each batt must be supported on two wall ties and must course with the ties. Care must be taken to ensure that the batts are kept free from mortar droppings and that all joints are butted together tightly. The first course of batts can be fixed below ground level and may have to be cut to give a level course for the next course to be built on. Cutting will also be needed to ensure a good fit and complete coverage at window and door openings, eaves level and gable verges. Non-rigid batts which fill the cavity are also fitted in a similar way and similar care must be taken with them. When building walls with cavity batts, the inner skin is built first up to the height of one course of batts (this is usually six courses of bricks or two courses of blocks). The batts are then fixed in position and the outer skin built up to this height, then the process is repeated. A board is placed on top of the batts when the inner skin of the wall is being built to prevent mortar droppings falling on them. Cutting of batts is quite easy using a long knife or trowel, although a hand saw may be used on some rigid board types. If the cavity insulation is not taken up into the apex of a gable end, a cavity tray d.p.c. must be built-in along the length of the gable wall immediately above the last course of insulation batts.

### Sills to openings

A sill at the bottom of a window opening provides a weather resistant feature, preventing water entering at this point and may also serve as a decorative feature to the building. There must be a weathertight joint between the window frame and the sill so that rain water will run off the face of the building after it has run down the window. A durable, sloping, weathered surface with a drip throating and a d.p.c. are the important points. Wood, brick, stone, concrete, steel, tiles and slates are all commonly used as sills.

Hardwood sills bedded on to the wall with mortar are likely to suffer from wet rot fairly early in their life (Fig. 100).

Brick sills may be built from purpose-made bricks (Fig. 101b) or from standard face bricks. The brick on edge projects from the wall face, forming a drip and closing the cavity. The top edges of the bricks fit into a groove in the timber frame and with a mastic seal forms a watertight joint. This type of sill may form a pleasing feature on the elevation

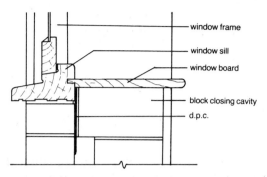

Fig. 100. Section of a wood window sill

of the building, but has a lot of joints which are a potential weakness. The sill is constructed by first bedding a brick at each end in the required position on a fairly stiff mortar mix. A line is then fixed across the front edge and the remaining bricks are pressed into place and kept to the line. Another line may be necessary along the back edge to ensure level work to bed the frame sill on. The cross joints must be trowelled on to each brick as full as possible so that there is no need to fill the joints afterwards as this would tend to disturb them.

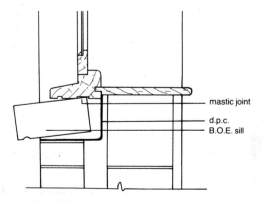

Fig. 101a. Brick on edge window sill section

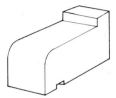

*Fig. 101b. Purpose-made bullnosed sill brick*

Stone and concrete sills are very similar, although stone sills are generally much thicker. The top surface is sunk and weathered to ensure quick run off of the water and a groove is cut or cast into the top where the wooden frame is bedded. On the end of the sills is a stooling which is built into the wall either side of the opening. Alternatively, the sill may be the exact width of the opening and not built in at the sides. Additional weather resistance is given by using a galvanized steel water bar set in mastic (Fig. 102).

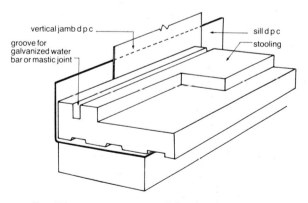

*Fig. 102. Concrete or stone sill detail with end stooling*

Steel sills are pressed-steel sheet which is galvanized and forms part of the steel window frame. This fixes over the

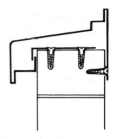

*Fig. 103. Section through steel sill*

brick or block walling and is clipped to brackets fixed with
screws (Fig. 103).

A tile sill can be made using a double course of tiles with
staggered joints laid on a stiff mortar bed using a similar
construction to the brick on edge method. Roofing tiles with
nibs form a good drip feature and can look attractive. The
half tiles made for the undereaves course or the ridge course
in roofing are most suitable for this work. The fixing nibs

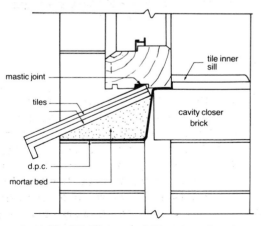

*Fig. 104. Two-course tile or slate sill*

must be cut off for the second course to get a flush front edge. Purpose-made tiles can be obtained, but are mainly used for restoration work (Fig. 104).

Slate sills may be built of two courses of dressed slates as described for tiles, or purpose-made sawn and dressed slate sills similar to concrete may be used (Fig. 105).

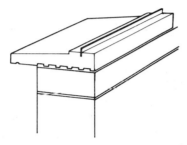

*Fig. 105. Purpose-made sawn and dressed slate sill*

The sill is a projecting feature which must be protected against possible damage from falling material during construction, using a piece of polythene sheet and a wood cover.

## Thresholds

Thresholds are situated at the bottom of a door opening in an external door. The threshold is subject to a great deal of wear and must prevent rain water getting into the building under the door. A pre-cast concrete type is available which has a trough with a grating and a drain-off pipe leading from it to take away any water which has found its way under the door (Fig. 106). Other thresholds have a stop cast or planted on for the door to close on to, or a patent threshold with a p.v.c. insert which seals the gap at the

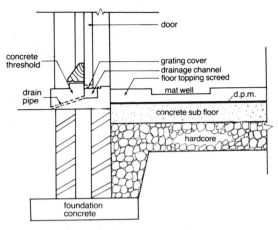

*Fig. 106. Section of a threshold*

bottom of the door. Like sills thresholds need protection during construction.

## Cutting and building gables

The gable ends are built either before any of the roof timber is set up or after roof timbers are complete.

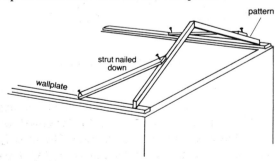

*Fig. 107. Pattern rafter fixed in place*

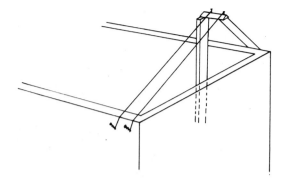

*Fig. 108. Gallows bracket*

When building the gables first it will be necessary to set up a pattern rafter (Fig. 107), or a gallows type bracket (Fig. 108). Lines are then fixed into the wall at the bottom and to the bracket at the top. These lines are used for marking the bricks for cutting and aligning them in position

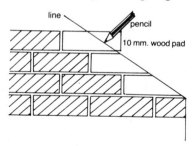

*Fig. 109. Marking the bricks for cutting*

(Fig. 109). The bricks to be cut are placed in position on a 10 mm piece of wood and marked with a pencil. The external face should be cut accurately with a bolster chisel, but the internal cut does not have to be so accurate. The gable is built up by plumbing at each end and racking back (Fig. 110). The wall is then built with a line as normal. The bricklayer must

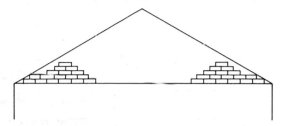

*Fig. 110. Building the gable*

be careful when setting up the courses to make sure that the cross joints on the work are kept plumb. Where the roof has an overhanging verge, the walling is built up under the timber work (Fig. 111). This is often difficult for the brick-layer who has to reach up under the woodwork, so a hard hat is a good protection for this work.

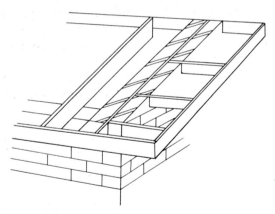

*Fig. 111. Overhanging verge and barge boards*

At the bottom of the gable a knee corbel may be featured to cover the end of the fascia and soffit and to give an architectural effect. Corbels can take several forms. A brick corbel is built out using the level on the bottom of each course and to line up the front edges (Fig. 112). The pro-

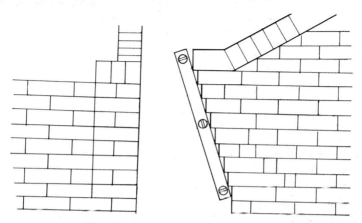

*Fig. 112. A brick knee corbel to a gable end*

jection of each course must not be more than quarter brick and the total projection should not be so great that the corbel becomes top heavy. A concrete or stone corbel is easier to build in and is just as effective (Fig. 113). Although elaborate brick and tile corbels are used as decorative features, they require considerable skill to construct.

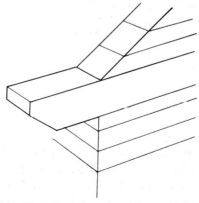

*Fig. 113. A stone or concrete corbel*

# 7

# Pavings and Steps

Paved areas and footpaths perform two functions. First they provide hard standing and walkways and secondly they can enhance the appearance of urban and country hard landscape.

Plain or coloured concrete paving flags are made in two standard sizes $600 \times 600$ mm and $900 \times 600$ mm and two thicknesses 37 and 50 mm. Flags must be stacked on edge (Fig. 114) and as near to the work area as possible. The

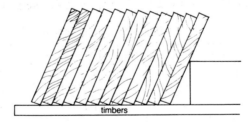

timbers

*Fig. 114. Flags stacked on site*

finished paving will only be as good as the foundation work – a firm well drained foundation is achieved by a layer of well compacted hardcore. The flags are laid on a bed of sand screeded level which averages 50 mm thick. A rubber mallet is used to tamp the flags on to the sand bed, but to compress the sand a club hammer and piece of wood can be used instead. Without the timber buffer a club hammer will damage or crack the flag. Flags can be bedded in cement mortar

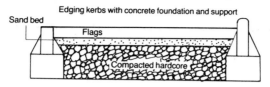

*Fig. 115. Cross section of a footpath*

on a concrete bed if vehicles are to run on them, but a sand bed is satisfactory for pedestrians (Fig. 115). The joints are 10 mm and are filled with 1:4 cement–sand mortar. A dry mix is brushed over the surface filling the joints, the mortar is then pressed down in to the joint using a small jointer or a piece of wood, and further mortar brushed over and pressed in until the joint is full and solid.

Crazy paving consists of pieces of broken flags laid in a random fashion and fitted into each other. The joints should be between 10 and 25 mm wide and are filled with mortar and trowelled in a similar way to rectangular flags (Fig. 116).

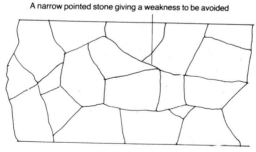

*Fig. 116. Crazy paving*

Concrete flags are available in various surface finishes such as exposed aggregate or rough textures imposed during moulding. Random size flags can be bonded to give a great variety of pleasing patterns, an example is shown Fig. 117. Paved areas must always be laid to falls, to run the rain

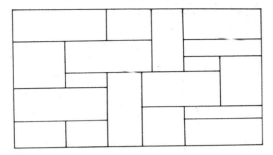

*Fig. 117. Random size paving stones*

water off. A tapered rule and spirit level can be used to give the required fall (Fig. 118).

Brick paving can be used to produce a feature in flag paving or as paving in its own right. Brick paviours need to be dense, hard wearing and frost resistant and special paviours are manufactured for this work, although a good quality brick can be used. The bricks are bedded on sand or

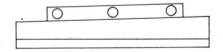

*Fig. 118. Tapered rule and level*

mortar in the same way as flags and jointed by the same method. They can be laid flat or on edge. Other paving materials are various concrete blocks and natural stones. Edging kerbs confine the sand and prevent erosion at the edge of the pavement. The kerbs are bedded with a semi-dry cement mortar 1:3 on a concrete foundation then backed with concrete (Fig. 115). The kerbs may be chamfered, square or round top and are 50 mm thick and 150 mm high. A number of bonding patterns used for flag and brick pavings are shown in Fig. 119. Where cutting is necessary the hammer and bolster chisel are used, but a much better

*Fig. 119. Bonding patterns for brick and flag paving*

job can be done by using a portable power saw. Curves are formed by taking a series of cuts and rounding off the points. An alternative bedding for footpaths is the 5 spot method Fig. 120.

Large areas of brick and concrete paving blocks are laid by hand on a carefully screeded sand bed using tight dry joints. Sand is scattered on top of the blocks and a flat-plate power vibrator is worked over the surface. This compacts the blocks evenly into the sand bed and shakes the sand into the joints, filling them tightly. Vehicle bearing drives and roadways can be constructed using this method and there are various shapes of interlocking blocks made for the purpose.

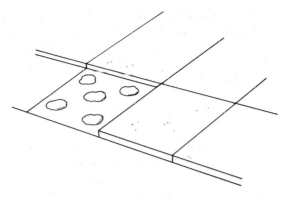

*Fig. 120. Lime 5 spot mortar bedding on compacted s  nd screen*

Thorough compaction of the foundation and the blocks is vital for success of these roadways.

Pre-cast concrete steps are built up on brickwork on a concrete foundation. The finished height of the top step has to be determined and the first step set at a level which will ensure that the flight finishes at the required height. The

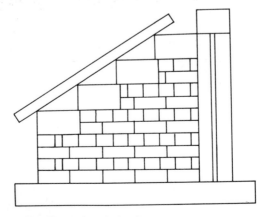

*Fig. 121. A short flight of pre-cast concrete steps*

treads and risers must be equal so that a person walking down will not trip. A straightedge should touch the nosings of all the steps (Fig. 121). As an alternative, steps can be built from flags which blend with the paving. They are bedded on a brick on edge course (Fig. 122).

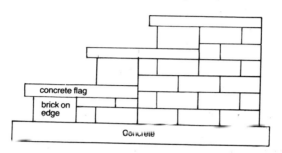

*Fig. 122. Steps constructed from flags*

The foundation must be deep enough to support the steps, a common failure is foundations that are too shallow. A pad foundation over the whole area of the steps will give a sound base if laid at the same depth as the main wall foundation.

# 8

# Freestanding walls and piers

A freestanding wall is one which is exposed on both sides and the top. It is not restrained at the top in any way or supported by any part of a structure. If built outdoors it would be a garden or boundary wall or a parapet wall. These walls are exposed to the weather on all sides, and must resist:

(A) saturation and drying;
(B) overturning by wind pressure;
(C) frost attack.

Usually these walls must look attractive and complement the urban or rural landscape as well as being functional. A good quality facing brick or facing block is essential. A coping must protect the top of the wall and prevent it being saturated. The walling must have a d.p.c. below the coping or the coping should be waterproof. Another d.p.c. at a minimum of 150 mm above ground level is required to prevent ground water rising through the brickwork.

Concrete copings are cast in metre lengths and must be bedded on to the wall with 1:3 cement–sand mortar. The end stones are bedded, and levelled in place with a spirit level, then a line is stretched tightly in order to align the stones in between. The copings are pressed down into position on the mortar bed by using a club hammer and a wooden dolly. The cross joints must be pressed full of mortar making sure that the throating is kept continuous through the joint. Fig. 123 shows various copings.

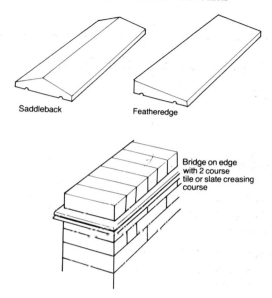

Saddleback

Featheredge

Bridge on edge
with 2 course
tile or slate creasing
course

*Fig. 123. Copings*

A brick on edge coping needs to be made from good quality weather resistant bricks, but the excessive number of vertical cross joints is a weakness and can allow water into the wall. Also a brick on edge coping does not project and form a drip to run the water off. A better job is done by setting the brick on-edge on top of the projecting double course of clay tiles or slates. The slate or tile courses are laid on a thin bed of 1:3 cement–sand mortar in two courses with staggered joints.

When building a brick on edge coping it is essential to make sure the joints are full and solid with the mortar spread evenly on the brick which is pressed firmly home against the next brick. The coping is returned at an angle by cutting the bricks as shown in Fig. 124. The corner bricks must be marked and cut, then put together dry to make sure they

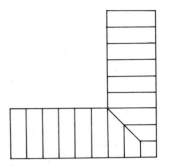

*Fig. 124. Plan of a square return to a brick on edge coping*

will fit. Brick on edge copings can be varied by setting bricks on end as shown in Fig. 125. This makes the coping on a low wall more difficult for children to run along and play

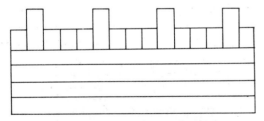

*Fig. 125. A coping of brick on edge and on end*

on. When a boundary wall is built on a sloping site, the top of the wall can be stepped or ramped as shown in Fig. 126. The mitre cuts are equal angles to fit together.

Garden wall bonds were specially developed for boundary walls faced both sides. They are adapted from English and Flemish bonds, but use less headers. Fig. 127 shows the face appearance of English and Flemish garden wall bonds. Less headers mean less cross joints and in the case of clay bricks which are of variable length, it means that fewer headers of

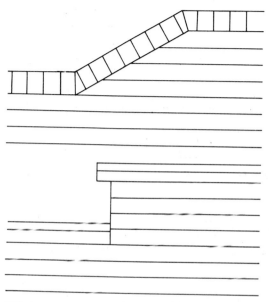

*Fig. 126. An example of a brick on edge ramp and a stepped coping*

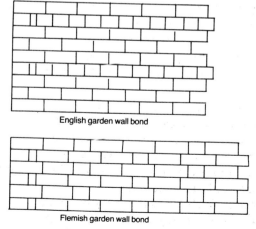

English garden wall bond

Flemish garden wall bond

*Fig. 127. Garden wall bonds*

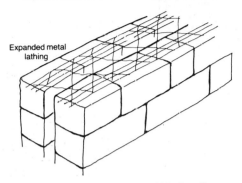

*Fig. 128. A double sided block wall*

the same length have to be sorted to give a good appearance on both sides of the wall.

Facing blocks are often faced only on one side and to produce a boundary wall faced both sides it has to be built in two skins tied together with expanded metal lathing (Fig. 128).

### Screen walls

These are built with blocks which are pierced or brick bonds which leave openings and give a honeycombed open work effect which is particularly attractive in gardens, but can also be effective indoors. The pre-cast concrete blocks are manufactured $300 \times 300 \times 100$ mm thick in a variety of patterns (Fig. 129) and are built with piers of pilaster blocks to stabilize the wall (Fig. 130). The wall is then finished off with a coping (Fig. 131). Screen blocks have straight joints and the mix should be 1:5 cement–mortar with a plasticizer. Expanded metal reinforcement in the bed joints may have to be used for large panels. These blocks are not easy to keep plumb and level and care is needed to spread a very

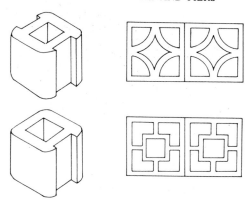

*Fig. 129. Examples of screen blocks*

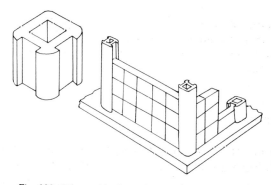

*Fig. 130. Pilaster blocks and example of screen wall*

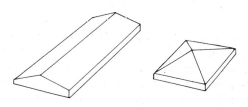

*Fig. 131. Coping and pilaster capping*

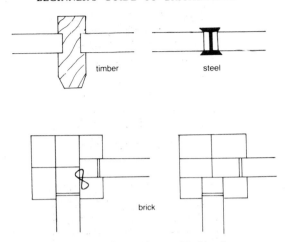

*Fig. 132. Supporting screen block walls*

even bed. The pilasters are built first and the blocks built into the groove. Setting out must be accurate as these blocks cannot be cut, corners must be square and wall lengths have to be multiples of the block size. Internal panels of screen blocks are often built into timber supporting frames or occasionally brickwork (Fig. 132). Screen walls of bricks are perhaps more versatile and various sizes of wall can be produced, the brick cutting being no problem. Usually brick walls are more stable than the concrete blocks, angles other than 90° can be built, including curved walls. The bricks are built as Flemish bond without the header in the same way as a honeycombed sleeperwall or holes can be left to form a pattern as shown by the examples in Fig. 133. Jointing and pointing are carried out on screen walls in the same way as for any other walls. It must be remembered that screen block walls are not load bearing and should not be expected to carry anything other than the lightest of loads.

Screen blocks can be cast rather than bought from a

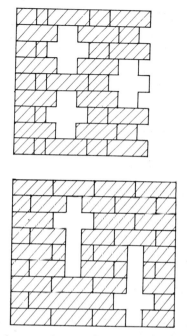

*Fig. 133. Perforated screen walls in bricks*

manufacturer by purchasing a mould. This mould will give good service and if used properly satisfactory blocks can be made. The manufacturers' instructions must be followed and a fairly dry mix used. Making blocks by hand is time consuming and not really practical for a builder but the d.i.y. enthusiast may find this worthwhile.

## Isolated detached piers

Piers are not easy to keep plumb on all sides because plumbing one side will affect the opposite side. The bed joints

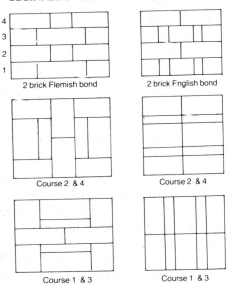

Fig. 134. Bonding brick isolated piers

and cross joints must be spread and applied evenly to the required thickness so that the bricks or blocks can be laid with precision and pressed into position with the minimum of force. Frequent use of the spirit plumb will be needed on all corners. The bricks will be spread out and the pier will

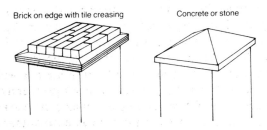

Fig. 135. Pier cappings

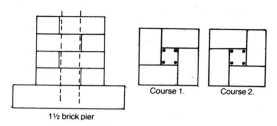

1½ brick pier

*Fig. 136. Reinforced brick pier*

get bigger if mortar is pushed down into the internal joints and it will not be possible to press it back into size. The pier will need a capping to resist the weather and prevent water penetration in the top. Examples of bonding piers are shown in Fig. 134 and of cappings in Fig. 135. The one and a half brick square pier can be built hollow and filled with concrete, which can be reinforced by rods cast into the concrete foundation (Fig. 136) for extra stability.

## Attached piers

Attached piers are used to add strength to walls, stiffening them and giving extra stability, thus allowing a thin wall to be built to a greater height than would otherwise be possible. Fig. 137 shows the bonding of a number of different attached brick piers. Some blockwork piers are shown in Fig. 138.

Mixing bricks and blocks in the same wall and pier is bad practice because the materials expand and contract differently and stress between different materials will often cause cracks. A brick wall must have brick piers and a block wall block piers. When building attached piers each course of the pier is built at the same time as each course of the wall.

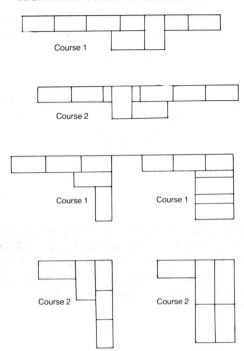

*Fig. 137. Bonding examples of attached piers in brickwork*

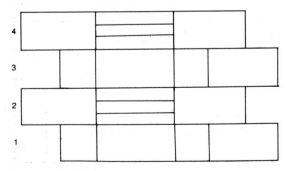

*Fig. 138. Examples of attached piers in blockwork using standard blocks*

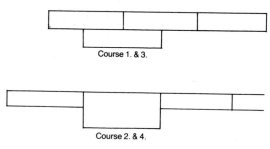

Course 1. & 3.

Course 2. & 4.

*Fig. 138. (Continued)*

Another form of attached pier is one which terminates a wall, which is usually found on a boundary wall with a gate pier attached at the end. The pier is built first with the attached wall racked back. Examples of brickwork are shown in Fig. 139 and of blockwork in Fig. 140.

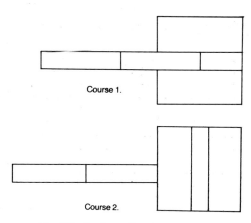

Course 1.

Course 2.

*Fig. 139. Garden wall with end pier*

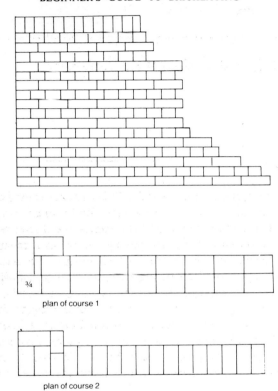

plan of course 1

plan of course 2

*Fig. 140. Attached terminal pier in brickwork*

# 9

# Patio and flower boxes

**Setting out**

The dimensions of patios and flower boxes are decided either by the limitations of space available or by measuring the number of flags required and the size of the flower boxes. The position and level of the paving and boxes is measured and marked on the house wall to ensure the required relationship with the existing building. Using a builder's square, a straightedge and a tape measure, a wood peg is driven at each front corner with a nail in the top to fix the exact position of the front edge. Diagonal measurements are taken to check that the patio will be square. Profiles can now be set up on pegs as described in Chapter 4 for the front corners and nailed to the wall for the back corners (Fig. 141).

The top soil is removed over the site area and the foundation trenches are dug out, the depth being determined by gauging down from the finished height, pegs being driven in to mark the concrete foundation level (Fig. 142). Concrete mixed at 1:2:4 or 1:6 with 'all in' gravel is poured and well tamped to the level of the pegs. Where available, a small hand fed mixer is suitable for this job. The quantity required would be too small for ready-mixed concrete to be economical. When the concrete has hardened, the foundation wall is built using common brick or dense aggregate concrete blocks below ground level. The facing work must start just

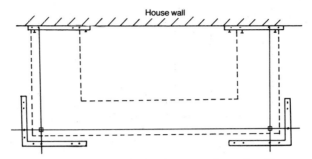

*Fig. 141. Setting out the foundation trenches and profiles*

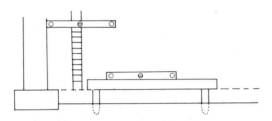

*Fig. 142. Levelling the foundation concrete pegs*

below ground level. Fig. 143 shows the arrangement of Flemish bonding to brickwork of one of the front corners. An alternative arrangement of bonding using rock-faced blockwork is shown in Fig. 144. It is sometimes more difficult to tie-in walls built with blocks, and to make a satisfactory job expanded metal or wire wall ties may be needed to secure the walls together. When the walling to the flower boxes and the front wall is complete and has hardened, the hardcore consisting of broken stone or old broken brick is packed and consolidated with a heavy hammer to compact as much as possible. This is then blinded

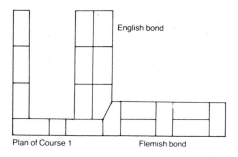

English bond

Plan of Course 1                    Flemish bond

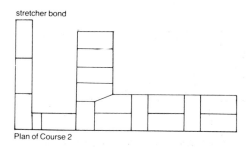

stretcher bond

Plan of Course 2

*Fig. 143. The Flemish bond arrangement of brickwalling to front corner of flower box and patio*

with sand which is screeded and tamped to the required level. The flags are laid on the sand bed starting at the back left-hand corner, using a piece of wood to ensure a 10 mm joint. The flags are consolidated by using a lump hammer and a piece of wood. The wooden straightedge is used to ensure that the flags are even and straight along the front of each course. A fall to the front edge can be formed by using a tapered straightedge or by baying the flags at each side and ensuring they have an even fall using a wooden

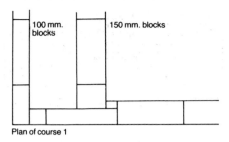

100 mm. blocks    150 mm. blocks

Plan of course 1

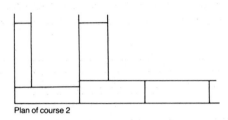

Plan of course 2

*Fig. 144. Bonding the front corner of the patio in blocks*

straightedge (Fig. 145). The joints in the flags are pointed with a 1:3 mortar mixed fairly dry and well pressed into the joints. The dry joint between the house wall and the patio has to be sealed using a mastic gun or a self-propelling cartridge. The steps have to be set out by measuring down from the finished patio level and out from the front of the wall to get the position of the bottom step (Fig. 146).

The space behind the brick step is filled with hardcore and the required number of steps built up. Each step must be levelled both ways and the nosings of the steps lined up with a level or straightedge (Fig. 147). Industrial leather gloves should be worn when lifting paving stones and care

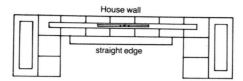

*Fig. 145. Plan of patio paving and flower boxes*

taken to avoid trapping fingers. A flag lifter which grips the side of the flag when the handles are lifted is the safest method and this can be hired or bought for the job. Fig. 148 shows a method of placing the last flag in an area of paving by hand. This method can be used to replace a broken flag

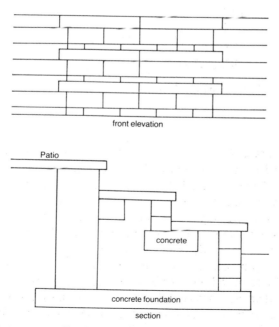

*Fig. 146. Details of steps to patio*

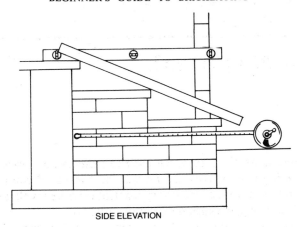

SIDE ELEVATION

*Fig. 147. Checking the step dimensions*

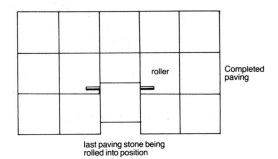

last paving stone being
rolled into position

*Fig. 148. Placing the last flag*

# 10

# Pointing a wall

Repointing an old wall which has been affected by years of weathering will improve the resistance of the brickwork to rain and frost, reduce the water penetration of the wall, and enhance the appearance if done properly.

The existing joints must be raked out to a depth of at least 15 mm. This may be easy in an old lime-mortar wall, but may need a club hammer and plugging chisel in harder mortars (Fig. 149). Work on an area of about a square metre

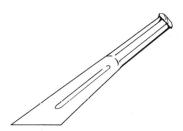

*Fig. 149. Plugging or jointing chisel*

at a time taking out the vertical joints first then the bed joints. The joints are then brushed down to remove all dust particles and thoroughly wetted. The brickwork should be damp so that it does not absorb all the moisture out of the mortar. When the raking out is completed the repointing is carried out. The mortar should be of a similar strength to the walling. It is no good using a very strong cement and sand mix on a soft porous type brick in a lime mortar. The mortar is mixed in small quantities and accurate measurement of materials is necessary to ensure that the same mix is used every time. Sometimes a special sand must be used to produce a particular colour or perhaps colour pigments added. Bags of silver sand, or crushed stone dust, ideal for the small quantities required, can be bought from a builders' merchant.

The mortar should be semi-stiff as a wet mortar of bricklaying consistency will run and smudge the face of the bricks. Mortar is placed on the hand hawk and a small quantity pressed on to the back of the trowel (Fig. 150). The vertical joints are pointed first, the trowel being used to press the mortar firmly into the joint, making sure it is full. Then the bed joints are filled the same way (Fig. 151), working the trowel along the joint not across it. The joint is finished by

Fig. 150. Picking up mortar from a hand hawk with the pointing trowel

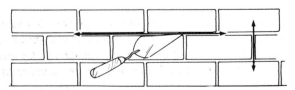

Fig. 151. Weather pointing with a trowel

applying the trowel at an angle for weather pointing or struck pointing (Fig. 152). Flush pointing is rubbed to take the rough edges off. This has to be done when the mortar has stiffened up, excessive rubbing will smudge the mortar into the face of the bricks. Recessed joints are ironed in with

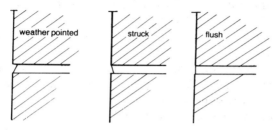

weather pointed    struck    flush

*Fig. 152  Sections of pointed joints*

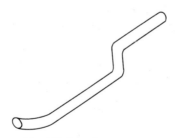

*Fig. 153. Round jointing iron*

a jointing iron (Fig. 153). Raked joints are formed with a scraper or with a roller jointing tool (Fig. 154). A light brushing over after the pointing will remove any rough edges which may remain.

The joint finish and texture will change the character of brickwork and blockwork so the profile of the joint has to be carefully selected to enhance the appearance. Coloured mortars are another way of changing the appearance of the joint.

The use of a trowel or jointing tool not only gives the

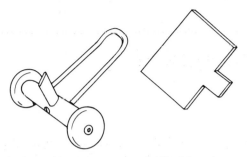

*Fig. 154. Joint scraper and roller joint raker*

profile, but pressing and ironing in the mortar makes it more weather resistant and durable. A round recessed jointer can be made easily from a piece of copper or steel tube or a small glass bottle like as aspirin bottle can be used. When galvanized metal buckets were in common use the handles made very good jointers and so this round type of jointing is commonly called bucket handle pointing. Recessed pointing is most successful where the bricks or blocks are of uniform square edges and an even 10 mm joint is maintained. Pointing open textured blockwork or rough texture facing bricks requires a lot of care to keep the mortar off the face and avoid filling the pores or smudging the faces.

# 11

# Circular paving

If the paving is surrounding an existing tree, a template will
be needed for setting out the circle. The template can be cut
out of hardboard or some similar thin sheet material and
used to mark out and build the first or inner course as shown
in Fig. 155.

If the centre is clear then a trammel rod can be used. A
steel pin driven into the ground at the centre or a wooden
peg with a nail in the top can be used to turn the trammel
on. The trammel rod ensures that the bricks radiate from
the centre (Fig. 156).

The circle is marked on the ground by scratching a mark,

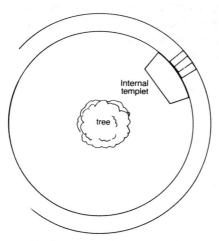

*Fig. 155. Using an internal templet*

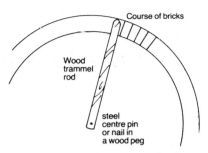

*Fig. 156. Using a trammel rod*

the area is then dug out to the depth required for a hardcore base which is rammed down to the required level. If a large circle is being built, pegs may have to be driven in and levelled to ensure that the hardcore is spread evenly.

The first inner circle of bricks is bedded in cement mortar spread on to the sand-blinded hardcore. Each brick is jointed with mortar and pressed down firmly on to the mortar bed. The templet or the trammel is used to ensure the accuracy of the circle taking care to align the bricks along the radius of the circle – this can be done with the trammel rod or by squaring from the templet.

After completing the first ring, the second ring can be laid on a dry sand cement mix, each brick is hammered down firmly using a lump hammer and a piece of wood to protect the surface. Constant use of the spirit level will be needed to keep the work level. Further rings can now be laid in the same way until the required number is reached. The last outer ring is bedded on a semi-stiff mix and the joints filled with mortar. The joints of the inner brick rings are filled with a dry cement–sand mix brushed in and pressed with a jointer, then filled flush by a second brushing of the mix. The brickwork joints will be vee-shaped in order to obtain the curve, obviously the small radius curves will be more difficult to lay than the larger radius rings.

# 12

# Garden seat and barbecue

The setting out of these garden features (Fig. 157) will have to be related to an existing fence, path, wall or building. The concrete base and foundation raft is rectangular in each case

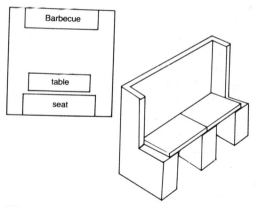

*Fig. 157. Plan of suggested layout and pictorial view of seat*

and can be marked out on the ground with a wooden square and straightedge, then dug out to the required depth. Profiles are not necessary for small items like this and a single level peg will be sufficient. The concrete slab must be tamped to 75 mm below the ground level so that the finished brick paving will be level with the ground (Fig. 158).

The brickwork can now be set out on the concrete base,

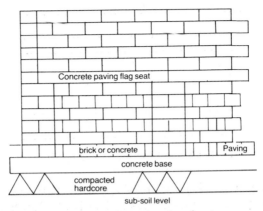

*Fig. 158. Front elevation of seat*

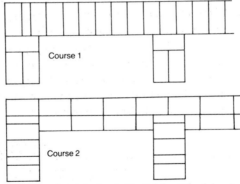

*Fig. 159. Plans showing the bonding in English bond for the seat and barbecue*

the first course laid as the bonding plan (Fig. 159). The end
piers are then built. Although this wall is short, a string line
will be a necessary guide to build it properly. The centre pier
is built one course at a time with each course of the back
wall (Fig. 160). It is best to complete the brickwork and let
it set before bedding on the concrete flags which will form
the seat.

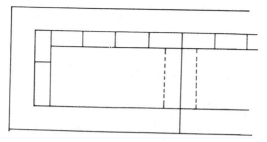

*Fig. 160. Plan showing top course of seat back*

The barbecue (Fig. 161) is of similar construction to the seat. The pre-cast concrete flags and the back of the barbecue must be lined with fire-bricks 75 mm thick on the base, 50 mm thick on the back. These bricks are laid in fireclay and water mixed to a very soft mortar consistency which is spread thinly. The end and side face of the brick is buttered with the fireclay mortar and the brick firmly pressed on to the bed. The joint thickness should be 3 mm and solidly packed with mortar. The bars of the grill are set 150 mm maximum above the charcoal bed – standing them on legs is better than building them into the brickwork.

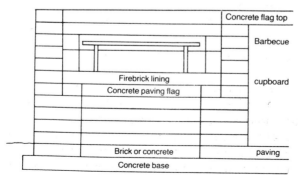

*Fig. 161. Front elevation of barbecue*

To the right of the barbecue a store cupboard for charcoal etc., with a concrete flag top would have a pair of wooden doors and could have a timber or concrete flag shelf.

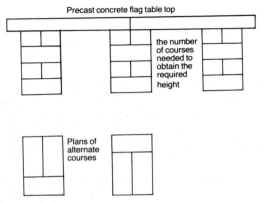

*Fig. 162. Detail of table*

The table is of similar construction, the three, one-and-a-half-brick piers being built on the concrete bed with two concrete flags bedded on after the brickwork has set (Fig. 162).

To complete the feature the paving has to be laid. Brick paving with a mortar bed on a compacted hardcore base would be very suitable for this and easily built around and under the features. Paving flags of any type will be a bit more difficult to place under the features and will involve more cutting and fitting to the piers.

# 13

# Feature fireplace

A fireplace can be a very effective feature and greatly enhance an otherwise ordinary room. It can be built from a great variety of materials, natural stones of all kinds, artificial reconstructed stone, split face and aggregate-faced concrete blocks, as well as the great variety of bricks available.

Many manufacturers supply kits of parts all numbered complete with everything needed to build the fireplace. Sets of partly made units are also available to build fireplaces and these may be easier for the beginner to use.

When purchasing in kit form it is essential to check the dimensions carefully to be certain that the finished work will fit the space available and will be a suitable scale for the room. If the standard dimensions offered by the manufacturer do not fit your requirements most will supply a special kit made up to your design and dimensions. The kit arrives with a key drawing and all the items numbered so that it can be assembled properly, the mortar is a dry ready mix which only needs water added. Some kits have parts of the fireplace ready-built in sections which have to be set up, fixed, and jointed together while other kits have all the components separate. The first stage is to unpack and check that all components are present and undamaged, usually there is a checklist enclosed. The first course should then be set out dry, measuring the joints and making sure of a good fit. Then proceed to build the feature, regularly checking plumb, level and gauge, remembering that very small errors will be obvious in a feature of this kind.

To design and build your own feature, start with a sheet of squared paper, any sheet of graph paper will do or a grid of lines can be lightly drawn on paper at say 5 mm intervals. Some rough sketches including any fixed dimensions will be very useful and will enable you to arrange random sized components to the best advantage. The drawing on the squared paper will then show the layout to scale and can be used to determine the quantities of each item required. If regular size materials such as bricks are to be used, the plotting of the bond on the paper will be fairly easy and

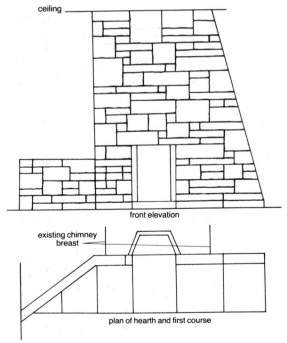

*Fig. 163. Fireplace feature in random size units*

the estimate of the number required fairly straightforward. Varied size materials are more difficult, but if the bonding arrangement has been plotted carefully an accurate estimate of each size can be made. A random size material such as natural stone is usually sold by the square metre so that the area will need to be taken from the dimensions available.

Random size stones and blocks should be laid out on the floor so that the bonding arrangement can be set out properly.

The example shown in Fig. 163 is a room feature built in random size reconstructed stone or split-face concrete blocks. Because a feature wall is very heavy the foundation

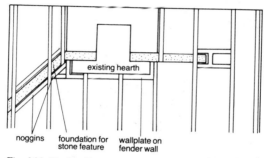

existing hearth

noggins    foundation for    wallplate on
stone feature    fender wall

*Fig. 164. Timber floor adjustments with right angle joists*

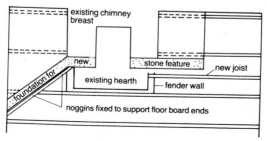

existing chimney breast

new

stone feature

new joist

foundation for

existing hearth

fender wall

noggins fixed to support floor board ends

*Fig. 165. Timber floor adjustments with parallel joists*

will have to be considered. If the room has a solid concrete floor this should be quite strong enough to support the work, but a timber floor will not. In both cases the first step is to mark out the plan on the floor using a carpenter's pencil. If the floor is timber then the floor boards must be taken up along the line of the wall and a foundation wall built. This foundation must be built up from the oversite concrete and carried around the joist ends if the joists run at right angles to the new wall (Fig. 164). If the joists are parallel with the wall then a new joist would have to be inserted just in front of the new wall (Fig. 165).

The angled wing would also have to be set out and the floorboards cut so that the foundation wall can be built up to floor level, cutting around joists as before. The ends of the floorboards will have to be supported by fixing noggins between the joists (Figs. 164 and 165).

The battered (sloping) end to the feature can be kept to a true line by fixing a straightedge firmly at the required angle. The blocks at that end are either purpose-made or may be cut and dressed as required. Some pre-cast blocks may not be suitable for cutting, so if purpose-made blocks are not obtainable an alternative is to step each course back by a few millimetres.

# 14

# Garage and utility room

Constructing a garage or any similar small building needs planning permission and Building Regulations approval in the same way as any other building. The garage and utility room shown in Fig. 166 is a facing brick structure with a tiled roof, concrete floor, and driveway.

The setting out and construction is the same as for a larger building. The corners of the building and the driveway are measured and marked by pegs. The top soil is excavated from the site to a depth of between 150 and 300 mm depending on the amount of cultivation the soil has had. Any shrubs or trees which will be very close to the building will have to be moved and old footpaths broken up and removed. The access to the site may have to be broken through an existing boundary wall, fence or hedge. The soil may be reuseable on the garden and other material could possibly be used for hardcore, but if the excavated and demolished material is not suitable for use it should be loaded into a skip and removed from the site. The foundation profiles must now be set up using the method shown in Chapter 4 and the foundation trenches excavated, the spoil removed and loaded into the skip.

To give access to the work and provide a hard standing for materials, the hardcore must be spread, levelled and compacted over the drive area. One method of ensuring that the hardcore is compacted to the correct level is to drive a number of pegs over the area, levelling them with a spirit

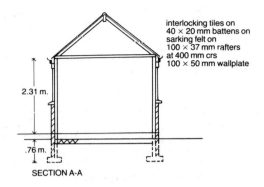

interlocking tiles on
40 × 20 mm battens on
sarking felt on
100 × 37 mm rafters
at 400 mm crs
100 × 50 mm wallplate

2.31 m.

.76 m.

SECTION A-A

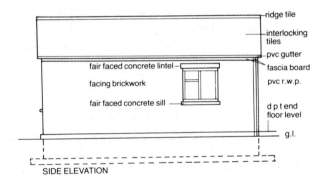

ridge tile

interlocking tiles

pvc gutter

fair faced concrete lintel

fascia board

facing brickwork

pvc r.w.p.

fair faced concrete sill

d p t end floor level

g.l.

SIDE ELEVATION

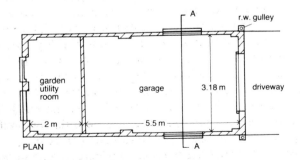

A

r.w. gulley

garden utility room

garage

3.18 m

driveway

2 m

5.5 m

PLAN

A

Fig. 166. Plans of garage and utility room

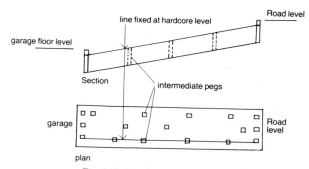

*Fig. 167. Level pegs for hardcore*

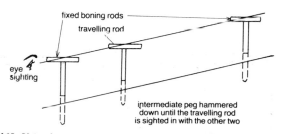

*Fig. 168. Using boning rods to set intermediate pegs at the correct height*

level and straightedge. If the driveway has a fall then a line stretched from a peg at one end to a peg at the other will enable intermediate pegs to be driven giving the correct fall (Fig. 167). Another method of ensuring an even fall would be to use boning rods and eyesight as shown in Fig. 168. The hardcore must be firmly compacted, a plate vibrator is the best machine for the inexperienced person to use as it can be handled similar to a hovermower. The top surface of the hardcore should be blinded (filled with fine material). The driveway area can then be used to stock material for building the garage and for mixing of mortar and concrete.

Because the concrete is required in three stages in fairly small quantities it will probably be more economical to mix it on site rather than buy ready-mixed concrete, but this will depend on the minimum load that the ready-mix depot will supply and the haulage distance between the depot and the work.

The foundation concrete is mixed, poured, compacted, and levelled, as described in Chapters 2 and 4. Building regulations require this concrete to be at least 150 mm thick and the width will depend on the type of subsoil. The local authority building control officer will have inspected the excavated trench before concreting starts and indicated any additional work that may be required if the subsoil is in very poor condition.

When the concrete has hardened sufficiently the brick substructure walls are built up to the d.p.c. level. A good quality weather resistant brick and mortar is required below the d.p.c. because this work will be permanently damp and liable to frost damage. The use of profiles and ranging lines for this work is shown in Chapter 4. The bonding of attached piers may give some problems. Suggested bonding arrangements are shown in Fig. 137. Because of the cutting involved these piers are often built with some straight joints which are tied together with wire ties or expanded metal (Fig. 169). This is often considered as strong as using a number of cut pieces to achieve acceptable bonding. The walls are now built up remembering to set out the door openings two brick courses below the finished floor level. The walling is built up to a suitable scaffold height, taking the corners up first and filling in the brickwork as described in Chapter 3. It is

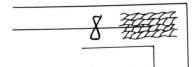

*Fig. 169. Use of wire wall ties or expanded metal*
*instead of bonding through an attached pier*

best to work from the outside but sometimes this is not possible because of space limitations due to, say, garden features, shrubs or trees. In this case the building will have to be done from the inside – this is called working overhand – and means that plumbing of the external angles is a bit more difficult. The line is still fixed on the outside if that is the face side. Trestle or any independent frame scaffolding would be suitable for this job, the important point is to make certain the feet of the scaffold are set on a firm secure base and are not going to sink into soft ground when the platform is loaded with bricks. The brickwork is completed up to eaves level, door and window frames being set up and built-in as described in Chapter 6. The gable ends have to be cut at the correct angle either by setting up pattern rafters or lines as shown in Chapter 6. A second lift of scaffolding will probably be required to build the gables.

Although carpentry is not part of this book, the roof work will be discussed in order that the reader will be able to understand the construction. The pitch or slope of the roof will be determined by the type of roof covering that is to be fixed. Some tiles and most slates need a pitch of 40° while other tiles need a pitch down to 20°, the manufacturer's catalogue information will give the pitch ideal for the type of tiles to be used. There are two methods of roof construction. Prefabricated roof trusses can be purchased; the manufacturer will need to know the span, pitch, and weight of roof covering. The joints in the trusses are either glued

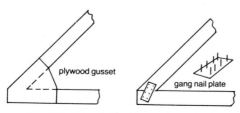

*Fig. 170. Joints in prefabricated roof trusses*

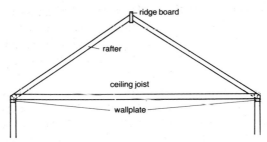

*Fig. 171. Traditional rafter roof*

plywood gussets or gang nail connecting plates (Fig. 170).
These trusses are set in position then nailed to the wallplate
and crossbraced to give rigidity.

The traditional rafter method of construction (Fig. 171),
is made up of precut rafters nailed at the top to the ridge-
board and at the bottom to the wallplate and the joist. This
forms a rigid triangular frame.

Both types of roof structure have to be fastened down
with galvanized or stainless-steel straps screwed to the truss
or rafter shown in Fig. 84. Also, in both cases the eaves have
to be completed with fascia and soffit boards. The roof can
then be completed by nailing the marking felt and battens
and fixing the slates or tiles. The ridge tiles and verges are
bedded and pointed in 1:3 cement–sand mortar.

The drainage work may be the most difficult job. Rainwater disposal may be through a combined sewer which
takes all waste and surface water, or a totally separate
surface water drain may be provided. Some local authorities
require a soakaway system if the conditions are suitable. If
there is any doubt over the rain water disposal then the local
authority building control officer should be able to advise.

Concreting the garage floor. The levelled compacted hardcore must be blinded with sand or similar fine material to a
thickness of between 25 and 50 mm to provide a suitable
bed for the polythene membrane – ensure that there are no

sharp projections which could puncture the membrane. The concrete will have to be screeded level, compacted, and surface finished. Levelling and compaction is achieved by bedding down two screeding boards as shown in Fig. 172. The concrete is then tamped and struck off using a sawing action until a fully conpacted layer with a true surface has been achieved. The screed boards have to be removed and the space filled with concrete either when the bulk of the floor is finished or they may be withdrawn gradually and the space filled as the work proceeds. The water cement ratio is critical as any surplus water is going to rise to the top and apart from giving a weak porous surface it makes trowelling of the finished surface impossible for a long time. Trowelling a finished, smooth surface is done from a wooden plank set in position above the concrete on a block or two bricks. The floor could be concreted when the foundation walls are up to floor level, in which case the levelling and compacting can be achieved using the tamping beam on the walls. This method may be easier, but the concrete would have to be protected when building the superstructure. A wooden float finish is probably best for a garage floor. This is achieved by rubbing the surface of the concrete with a wood or plastic hand float as the concrete is setting. Small imperfections are filled or rubbed in during this process and the result is a matt textured surface rather than the polished surface which is the result of steel trowelling. Surface finishing can only be

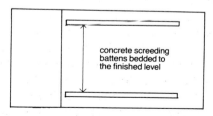

*Fig. 172. Outline plan of garage and screed boards*

applied when the concrete has reached the correct stage of setting. If the surface is too soft or too wet then the excess moisture can be removed by mopping up with newspaper or cloth. Do not allow water to run off the concrete as it will take some of the cement with it, resulting in a weak sandy surface. If the concrete has been mixed carefully and the water cement ratio is correct then the float finish can be carried out one to two hours after laying. The concrete must be cured as soon as the trowelling is finished and the best method would be to lay a polythene sheet on the surface. This will prevent the concrete drying out before hardening is complete. It should be kept in place for an extra 7 to 10 days in hot sunny weather.

*Concreting the driveway:* the first job is to fix edge formwork to act as shuttering and contain the edge of the wet concrete. It will also serve as the screed board for tamping and levelling the surface. Steel edge forms, which can be hired, are fixed in position by means of steel pins driven into the ground or hardcore base (Fig. 173). Timber forms are fixed and held in position by nailing them into wood pegs driven into the ground. To make sure the wooden or steel forms are straight, a line is set up to mark the finished level and concrete edge. The concrete is placed by shovel and tamped in the same way as for the garage floor, compacting and screeding it using the tamping beam.

The surface finish will depend on the needs of the owner,

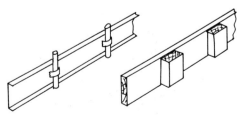

*Fig. 173. Steel and timber edge forms*

but a brushed surface formed by carefully dragging a stiff bristle broom back and forth across the concrete shortly after tamping gives a suitable surface for a driveway. As with the floor, a plank supported at each end on bricks or blocks and spanning the concrete about 200 mm above the surface will be suitable for walking on while surface finishing. A wood float finish can be given a decorative treatment by using a short straightedge and a bricklayer's jointing iron to make a crazy paving pattern on the surface. A ribbed surface is done with a jointing iron across the concrete at 150 mm intervals. The edges of the concrete can be finished off with a steel float to form a smooth trowelled margin or a special margin trowel can be used to smooth a curved edge next to the formwork (Fig. 174).

The most suitable way of curing this concrete in dry sunny weather is by spraying with water from a hosepipe. Because concrete is subject to initial drying shrinkage, and to thermal movement throughout its life, it will be necessary to incorporate movement joints if the driveway is more than 5 m long. To allow for expansion and contraction, the joint should be 12 mm wide and filled with a bitumen rubber joint compound. A liquid bitumen primer is brushed into the joint first, then the compound is heated and poured into the opening.

If a curved drive is necessary then flexible-steel edge forms are available which can be bent to the curve required and fixed with the steel pins in the same way as straight

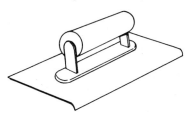

*Fig. 174. Concrete edging trowel*

ones. Alternatively, a hardboard or plywood strip can be used, but it needs a lot of pegs to support it and keep it in shape. Also, it is not as robust as steel and more care needs to be taken with the tamping beam.

A driveway that slopes down towards the garage will run water under the door into the garage unless means are taken to prevent it. The garage floor can be constructed 25 mm above the drive level and a small ramp formed at the entrance. Another method of dealing with this problem is to form a channel across the drive thus diverting the rainwater either side into gullies. The channel can be formed easily in the wet concrete with a milk bottle or a similar smooth cylindrical object; rub the concrete in the same way as trowelling the surface (Fig. 175). To prevent water being blown under the door in very windy conditions, a rubber door seal can be fitted to the bottom of the door.

The partition wall between the garage and the utility room should be built up along with the external walls if bonded

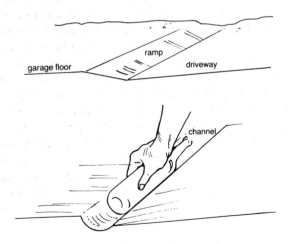

*Fig. 175. Ramp and channel to the front of the garage*

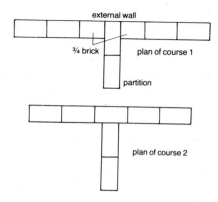

*Fig. 176. Tying in a Tee junction half brick wall*

in. Bonding the tee-junction is shown in Fig. 176 and the wall should be racked out from the external wall as the work proceeds or toothings projected. This wall can be taken up to scaffold level with the outer walls but the height will have to allow for the scaffold planks to pass right through. If the outer walls are in facing bricks and the partition wall is in a different type of brick, bonding it in will cause the tie-in brick to show on the outside as a different colour or texture. This is unacceptable in facing work, so a facing brick should be used or the partition can be tied into the outer wall using wire ties. These are built into every second course of the outer wall. The partition can then be built after the other walling is finished. Using this method of tying the partition results in no interference with the bonding pattern of the external wall face. The mortar joints of the partition and the wall surface should be flush pointed and lightly rubbed or brushed to a surface suitable for painting if that is desired.

# Index

Admixtures, 48
Air vents, 58–60
Arches, 76–9

Barbecue construction, 123–5
Bats (bricks), 19
Blocks:
    cutting, 45
    types, 20–5
Bolster chisel, 5–6
Bonding, 36–9, 98–9
Boning rods, 133
Brick cutting gauge, 6
Brick hammer, 7
Bricks:
    calcium silicate, 18
    classification, 16
    purpose made, 19–20
    quality, 16–17
    sizes, 18–19
    standard cut, 19
    types, 15–16

Cavity batten, 68
Cavity batts, insulation, 80–1
Cavity wall construction, 67
Cold weather working, 48
Comb hammer, 6–7
Concrete:
    curing, 33, 137
    floating, 32–3

foundations, 56, 133
laying, 32–4, 136–7, 137–9
materials, 34–5
mixing, 29–31
Copings, 96–7
Corbals, 88–9
Coring holes, 69
Corner line blocks, 8–9
Crazy paving, 91
Curing concrete, 33, 137
Cutting gauge, 5–6

Datum pegs, 51
Drainage, rainwater, 135–6
Drainage channels, 138–9

Edge forms, 137
English bond, 37–8
    garden wall, 98–9
Equipment, 11–14
Extrados, 79

Fireplace construction, 126–9
Flags, paving, 90–1
Flemish bond, 37–8
    garden wall, 98–9
Flettons (bricks), 15
Floating concrete, 32–3
Formwork, 32
    driveway, 137
Foundations, 55–60, 109, 133

Frames, fixing, 72, 74–5
Frogs, 17

Gable ends, 86–9
Garage construction, 130–7
Garden seat construction, 122–3
Gauge, brick cutting, 5–6
Gauge box, 30
Gauge rod, 14
Gauge staff, 45

Hardcore, laying, 131–2

Indents, 43, 46
Insulation, cavity batts, 80–1
Intrados, 79

Jointing tool, 116
Joints, brickwork, 116–18

Ladders, 64–5
Level pegs, 132
Line, bricklaying, 7–9
Line blocks, 7–9
Lintels, 70–3
London pattern trowel, 1
Lump hammer, 5–6

Mortar, 25–6
    handling, 1–5
    mixing, 26–9

Northern pattern trowel, 1

Pallettes, wooden, 74
Patio construction, 109–13
Paving, 90–4
    circular, 119–21
Paving stones, see flags
Piers:
    attached, 105–8
    detached, 103–5

Plasticizers, 26, 28
Plumb bob and line, 10–11
Plumb level, 9–11
Pointing, 116–18
Profile boards, 50–2, 54
Profile frame, 74–5
Putlog scaffold, 63–4

Racking back, 42
Rainwater drainage, 135–6
Reinforced lintels:
    brick, 73
    concrete, 71
Repointing, 115
Roof work, 134–5

Scaffolding, 61–6
Screeding boards, 136
Screen blocks, 101–2
Setting-out, 49–55
Shell bedding, 23
Shovel, 12
Sills, alternative, 81–5
Skutch, see comb hammer
Soldier arches, 71
Spirit level, 9–11
Spot board, mortar, 13
Square, builder's, 13–14
Squaring, 55
Squint (brick), 19
Starting work, 40
Stepped foundations, 56, 58
Steps, 94–5
    garden, 112–14
Stopped end, 41
Stretcher bond, 37
Surface finishing (concrete), 136–7

3:4:5 method (squaring), 55
Tamping, 32
Thresholds, 85–6

Tingleplate/tingles, 41, 44
Toothing, 42
Trammel rod, 119, 122
Trestle scaffolds, 61–3
Trowel:
  concrete edging, 138
  laying, 1–5

Utility room construction, 130–3

Voussoirs, 79
  cutting templet, 78

Wall:
  cavity, 67
  freestanding, 96
  partition, 140–1
  screen, 100–3
Wall bonding, 36–41
Wall openings, 70–1
Wall plate anchors, 70
Wall stability, 47
Wall ties, 67–8
Weather precautions, 47–8
Wheelbarrow, 12
Working overhand, 134

# Also available from Heinemann Newnes

## Central Heating

### A design and installation manual
### George Steele

Why are most heating systems designed over the last
20 years oversized, perhaps by as much as 50 per cent?
Why are radiator failures increasing? Why do so many
centrally-heated houses suffer from condensation?

George Steele has been running a nationally-known
heating company for nearly 20 years, during which time over
30,000 individual systems have been designed. From his
personal experience he advises you on many aspects of
heating not usually dealt with. He explains, for example, why
reflective panels behind radiators may not always achieve
their object, that if you have condensation on your kitchen
walls as well as the windows double glazing will not cure any
of it, that some electronic controls are a waste of money, that
anyone who advises you to drill holes in joists for pipe runs
has probably never installed a single system, and why it is so
important to understand how vapour transfer is linked to heat
transfer. There is also a method of estimating running costs
that will not become outdated with fuel price changes. These
and many other hints make George Steele's book invaluable
for everyone involved in heating: installers, DIYers and
students.

ISBN 0 408 01404 0

# Home Electrics

## Geoffrey Burdett

Home electrical work whether it is mending a fuse, fitting
a plug, adding a light or socket outlet or even completely
rewiring a house is within the capabilities of the keen
mechanically minded DIY man (or woman).

Electricity, because it flows along wires instead of through
pipes, cannot be seen or heard nor produces any smell, is
often regarded with great mystery. This is really a fallacy
since the actual wiring, fixing accessories and other
associated work is very much a practical and down to earth
exercise requiring no physics degree nor a college diploma.
Most of the work is non-electrical and consists of lifting
floorboards, drilling holes and fixing cables and boxes.

This is one of a series of books produced by writers from
DIY magazine, and has been thoroughly revised in 1986 by
W. Turner in accordance with the latest regulations.

ISBN 0 408 00245 X

Resources.

Resonses.